Foreward

The Way Through is not a ty
all. At A Plain Account we
decided that we wanted to
than providing an exegetic
The Way Through seeks to ig.

...............to come to your own
reflections on the Scriptures. This is a Spiritual Guide that directs you
through the Scriptures as well as a handful of curated creative mediums in
order to help you come to the reflection that God has for you. In this way *The
Way Through* is an invitation.

The elements that make up each day of this guide are simple: a scripture
(*Lectio Divina*), an art piece (*Visio Divina*), a poem or piece of prose (*Poema
Divina*), a song (*Audio Divina*), some reflection questions (*Daily Examen*), then
a prayer. Each day is intended to be pursued at the pace that is appropriate
for you. Some days you may only reflect a few minutes, but other days your
imagination may be consumed by what God is saying to you.

Each week begins with an encouraged practice or habit to be taken up that
week. These practices are a way to acknowledge our embodied faith; that
what we do and how we do it shape what we believe about God and our
neighbors.

This resource also seeks to blur the lines between sacred and secular. As a
Wesleyan resource, we hope this guide can emphasize God's prevenient
grace, the grace that goes before us, the grace that pervades all of existence.
To this end, there are songs, poems, and art piece that are explicitly sacred.
There are others that aren't. As Dostoevsky said, "Beauty will save the
world." And we believe beauty, in all of its forms, points us back to a
beautiful creator. As you journey through each day's collection, listen to
what God is saying to you, even if the piece isn't explicitly sacred. It may
help to even pull the lyrics up for the songs. (Especially for Saturday of the
Fifth Week of Lent… Just a heads up, the song is a bit on the heavier side.)

To make it easier to listen to the daily songs we have created two playlists: one on Spotify and one on YouTube. Subscribe to the playlist on your preferred platform and listen to that day's song. They are listed in order so it should be easy to follow.

 Grace and Peace,

Rev. Danny Quanstrom

Founder, A Plain Account

*A playlist of each day's song has been compiled and is accessible with this QR code.

The Way Through Lent Playlist

Acknowledgments

We are pleased to present the fourth installment of *The Way Through*. Working with a wonderful father-daughter team, Jay and Alexandra Sunberg has been my pleasure. From the beginning, Jay and Alexandra approached *The Way Through* with a sense of serious contemplation, which is shown in the final product. That they have done so comes as no surprise. Jay, his wife, Teanna, and the rest of their family have been humble and faithful servants of Jesus Christ and his church at home and abroad.

For my part, I am looking forward to following Jay and Alexandra's lead as we move through Lent toward Jesus' death and resurrection, using the prayers, texts, songs, poems, and art they have curated for us. I am confident that Jay and Alexandra's work will help anchor us as we seek to navigate our chaotic world faithfully.

Grace and Peace,
Rev. Dr. Jason C. Buckwalter
The Way Through Editor and Discipleship Team Lead

Acknowledgments

We are pleased to present the fourth installment of *The Way Through*.
Working with a wonderful father-daughter team, Jay and Alexandra
Sunberg has been my pleasure. From the beginning, Jay and Alexandra
approached *The Way Through* with a sense of serious contemplation, which is
shown in the final product. That they have done so comes as no surprise. Jay,
his wife, Teanna, and the rest of their family have been humble and faithful
servants of Jesus Christ and his church at home and abroad.

For my part, I am looking forward to following Jay and Alexandra's lead as
we move through Lent toward Jesus' death and resurrection, using the
prayers, texts, songs, poems, and art they have curated for us. I am confident
that Jay and Alexandra's work will help anchor us as we seek to navigate our
chaotic world faithfully.

Grace and Peace,
Rev. Dr. Jason C. Buckwalter
The Way Through Editor and Discipleship Team Lead

THE WEEK OF
ASH WEDNESDAY

ASH WEDNESDAY

The Weekly Collect

Almighty and everlasting God, you hate nothing you have
made and forgive the sins of all who are penitent: Create and
make in us new and contrite hearts, that we, worthily
lamenting our sins and acknowledging our wretchedness,
may obtain of you, the God of all mercy, perfect remission
and forgiveness; through Jesus Christ our Lord, who lives
and reigns with you and the Holy Spirit, one God, for ever
and ever. *Amen.*

Lectio Divina
Joel 2:1-2, 12-17

¹ Blow the trumpet in Zion;
    sound the alarm on my holy mountain!
Let all the inhabitants of the land tremble,
    for the day of the Lord is coming, it is near—
² a day of darkness and gloom,
    a day of clouds and thick darkness!
Like blackness spread upon the mountains,
    a great and powerful army comes;
their like has never been from of old,
    nor will be again after them
    in ages to come.

¹² Yet even now, says the Lord,
    return to me with all your heart,
with fasting, with weeping, and with mourning;

[13] rend your hearts and not your clothing.

Return to the Lord your God,

    for he is gracious and merciful,

slow to anger, abounding in steadfast love,

    and relenting from punishment.

[14] Who knows whether he will not turn and relent

    and leave a blessing behind him,

a grain offering and a drink offering

    for the Lord your God?

[15] Blow the trumpet in Zion;

    consecrate a fast;

call a solemn assembly;

[16] gather the people.

Consecrate the congregation;

    assemble the aged;

gather the children,

    even infants at the breast.

Let the bridegroom leave his room

    and the bride her canopy.

[17] Between the vestibule and the altar,

    let the priests, the ministers of the Lord, weep.

Let them say, "Spare your people, O Lord,

    and do not make your heritage a mockery,

    a byword among the nations.

Why should it be said among the peoples,

    'Where is their God?   " '

Visio Divina
"Prodigal Son" by Rembrandt (1669)

Poema Divina
"Come, Sinners, to the Gospel Feast" by Charles Wesley

1. Come, sinners, to the gospel feast;
let every soul be Jesus' guest.
Ye need not one be left behind,
for God hath bid all humankind.

2. Sent by my Lord, on you I call;
the invitation is to all.
Come, all the world! Come, sinner, thou!
All things in Christ are ready now.

3. Come, all ye souls by sin oppressed,
ye restless wanderers after rest;
ye poor, and maimed, and halt, and blind,

in Christ a hearty welcome find.

4. My message as from God receive;
ye all may come to Christ and live.
O let his love your hearts constrain,
nor suffer him to die in vain.

5. This is the time, no more delay!
This is the Lord's accepted day.
Come thou, this moment, at his call,
and live for him who died for all.

Audio Divina
"Come As You Are" by Crowder

Daily Prayer
Father, We come to this Ash Wednesday fully aware of our need for your
abundant mercy and grace. The ashes on our foreheads remind us of our
frailty and our complete dependence on you. We are reminded that from
dust we were created, and to dust we will return. Yet in this time between
the ashes, you have breathed life into us and formed us into your image. As
we walk this Lenten journey with you, we ask for your deeper work in our
lives. Strengthen our faith and shape us to become more like you. Amen.

THURSDAY

Lectio Divina
Psalm 91:1-2, 9-16

1 You who live in the shelter of the Most High,
   who abide in the shadow of the Almighty,
2 will say to the Lord, 'My refuge and my fortress;
   my God, in whom I trust.'

9 Because you have made the Lord your refuge,
   the Most High your dwelling-place,
10 no evil shall befall you,
   no scourge come near your tent.
11 For he will command his angels concerning you
   to guard you in all your ways.
12 On their hands they will bear you up,
   so that you will not dash your foot against a stone.
13 You will tread on the lion and the adder,
   the young lion and the serpent you will trample under foot.
14 Those who love me, I will deliver;
   I will protect those who know my name.
15 When they call to me, I will answer them;
   I will be with them in trouble,
   I will rescue them and honor them.
16 With long life I will satisfy them,
   and show them my salvation.

Visio Divina
"Guardian Angel" by Bernhard Plockhorst (1886)

Poema Divina
"Safe in the Haven of His Love" by William C. Dix

Safe in the haven of His love,
There is no storm, no rolling wave,
There is no peril from above,
No fear of ill from those who rave.

Refrain
Safe in the haven of His love,
Safe in the haven of His love,
Safe in the haven of His love,
Safe in the haven of His love.

Though tempest-tossed, and fiercely tried,
Beneath the dark and troubled sky,

Yet still we trust His grace to guide,
And keep us through the storm on high.

Refrain
He is our refuge and our stay,
Our shield from every threatening foe;
And though the night be dark and gray,
He will not let our faith forego.

Refrain
When earthly ties are torn away,
And all our hopes and dreams are gone,
Still we are safe where Christ will stay,
And find in Him our strength alone.

Audio Divina
"He Will Hold Me Fast" By Keith and Kristyn Getty

Daily Prayer
Father, we live in troubled times, surrounded by dangers. We confess that
the brokenness of this world is a result of our sin and rebellion against you.
Even so, we turn to you for shelter and protection from evil and harm. We
seek your help and guidance as we journey through life in this world. Thank
you for your constant presence and your gracious hand over us. Amen.

FRIDAY

Lectio Divina
Exodus 6:1-13

Then the Lord said to Moses, 'Now you shall see what I will do to Pharaoh: Indeed, by a mighty hand he will let them go; by a mighty hand he will drive them out of his land.'

2 God also spoke to Moses and said to him: 'I am the Lord. 3 I appeared to Abraham, Isaac, and Jacob as God Almighty, but by my name "The Lord" I did not make myself known to them. 4 I also established my covenant with them, to give them the land of Canaan, the land in which they resided as aliens. 5 I have also heard the groaning of the Israelites, whom the Egyptians are holding as slaves, and I have remembered my covenant. 6 Say therefore to the Israelites, "I am the Lord, and I will free you from the burdens of the Egyptians and deliver you from slavery to them. I will redeem you with an outstretched arm and with mighty acts of judgement. 7 I will take you as my people, and I will be your God. You shall know that I am the Lord your God, who has freed you from the burdens of the Egyptians. 8 I will bring you into the land that I swore to give to Abraham, Isaac, and Jacob; I will give it to you for a possession. I am the Lord. "'9 Moses told this to the Israelites; but they would not listen to Moses, because of their broken spirit and their cruel slavery.

10 Then the Lord spoke to Moses, 11' Go and tell Pharaoh king of Egypt to let the Israelites go out of his land. '12 But Moses spoke to the Lord, 'The Israelites have not listened to me; how then shall Pharaoh listen to me, poor speaker that I am? '13 Thus the Lord spoke to Moses and Aaron, and gave them orders regarding the Israelites and Pharaoh king of Egypt, charging them to free the Israelites from the land of Egypt.

Visio Divina
"His Mighty Hand" by Youngsung Kim (2017)

Poema Divina
"Under His Hand" by Anne C. Brontë

When shadows fall and night is near,
I rest beneath His hand;
No terror dares to hover near,
No storm can touch the land;
For in the darkness, calm I stand,
Secure beneath His hand.

Audio Divina
"Oh the Mighty Hand" by George Ting

Daily Prayer
Father, Thank you for your constant presence with us. Whatever burdens we face today, we reach for your outstretched hand, trusting in your guidance and protection. Free us from the chains we have bound ourselves with for too long. Thank you for Your loving care. Amen.

SATURDAY

Lectio Divina
Ecclesiastes 3:1-8

3 For everything there is a season, and a time for every matter under heaven:

2 a time to be born, and a time to die;

a time to plant, and a time to pluck up what is planted;

3 a time to kill, and a time to heal;

a time to break down, and a time to build up;

4 a time to weep, and a time to laugh;

a time to mourn, and a time to dance;

5 a time to throw away stones, and a time to gather stones together;

a time to embrace, and a time to refrain from embracing;

6 a time to seek, and a time to lose;

a time to keep, and a time to throw away;

7 a time to tear, and a time to sew;

a time to keep silence, and a time to speak;

8 a time to love, and a time to hate;

a time for war, and a time for peace.

Visio Divina
"Two Trees" by Katherine Blakeslee (2003)

Poema Divina

Great is Thy faithfulness, O God my Father

There is no shadow of turning with Thee

Thou changest not, Thy compassions, they fail not

As Thou hast been, Thou forever will be

Great is Thy faithfulness

Great is Thy faithfulness

Morning by morning new mercies I see

All I have needed Thy hand hath provided

Great is Thy faithfulness, Lord, unto me

Summer and winter and springtime and harvest

Sun, moon and stars in their courses above

Join with all nature in manifold witness

To Thy great faithfulness, mercy and love

Great is Thy faithfulness

Great is Thy faithfulness

Morning by morning new mercies I see

All I have needed Thy hand hath provided

Great is Thy faithfulness, Lord, unto me

Pardon for sin and a peace that endureth

Thine own dear presence to cheer and to guide

Strength for today and bright hope for tomorrow

Blessings all mine with 10, 000 beside

Great is Thy faithfulness

Great is Thy faithfulness

Morning by morning new mercies I see

All I have needed Thy hand hath provided

Great is Thy faithfulness

Great is Thy faithfulness

Great is Thy faithfulness, Lord, unto me.

Audio Divina
"Everything" by Tim Hughes

Daily Prayer

Father, in this life, we experience both great joy and deep despair. Yet through it all, your faithful presence remains our constant. As we enter this day, we do so with confidence, knowing that whether it brings hardship or joy, you are with us. Thank you for your gracious and unfailing care. Amen.

The Examen

1. What part of this week's devotional stood out to you? How did it impact your prayers and spiritual growth?
2. How did you handle challenges or moments of inspiration this week? Did they encourage you to take a new step in your faith?
3. How has this week's practice helped you understand Lent and prepare for Easter? Has your view of sacrifice, repentance, or forgiveness changed?
4. Are there any distractions or habits you'd like to let go of to make Lent more meaningful? How will you plan to create a peaceful, reflective space for yourself each day?

THE FIRST WEEK OF LENT

SUNDAY

Lectio Divina
Romans 10:8b-13

"The word is near you, in your mouth and in your heart" (that is, the word of faith that we proclaim), because if you confess with your mouth that Jesus is Lord and believe in your heart that God raised him from the dead, you will be saved. For one believes with the heart, leading to righteousness, and one confesses with the mouth, leading to salvation. The scripture says, "No one who believes in him will be put to shame." For there is no distinction between Jew and Greek; the same Lord is Lord of all and is generous to all who call on him. For "everyone who calls on the name of the Lord shall be saved.

"The End of History" by Francis O'Toole

Poema Divina

And can it be that I should gain

An interest in the Savior's blood

Died He for me, who caused His pain

For me, who Him to death pursued?

Amazing love! How can it be

That Thou, my God, should die for me?

Amazing love! How can it be

That Thou, my God, should die for me?

He left His Father's throne above
So free, so infinite His grace
Emptied Himself of all but love
And bled for Adam's helpless race
Tic mercy all, immense and free
For O my God, it found out me!

Amazing love! How can it be,
That Thou, my God, should die for me?

Long my imprisoned spirit lay,
Fast bound in sin and nature's night
Thine eye diffused a quickening ray
I woke, the dungeon flamed with light
My chains fell off, my heart was free
I rose, went forth, and followed Thee

Amazing love! How can it be
That Thou, my God should die for me?

No condemnation now I dread
Jesus, and all in Him, is mine
Alive in Him, my living Head
And clothed in righteousness divine
Bold I approach the eternal throne
And claim the crown, through Christ my own

Amazing love! How can it be
That Thou my God, should die for me?
Amazing love! How can it be
That Thou my God, should die for me?

Audio Divina

"Call Upon The Lord" by Elevation Worship

Daily Prayer
Father, thank you for the gift of salvation we have received through your son Jesus Christ. Help us to live in your grace and grow in our faith. We lift up those who are living outside of your care. We pray that you would send your Holy Spirit to them now, revealing your love in a way that is meaningful and transformative for them. Amen.

MONDAY

The Weekly Collect

Almighty God, whose blessed Son was led by the Spirit to be
tempted by Satan: Come quickly to help us who are assaulted
by many temptations; and, as you know the weaknesses of
each of us, let each one find you mighty to save; through
Jesus Christ your Son our Lord, who lives and reigns with
you and the Holy Spirit, one God, now and for ever. *Amen.*

Lectio Divina

1 Chronicles 21:1-17

21 Satan stood up against Israel, and incited David to count the people of
Israel. **2** So David said to Joab and the commanders of the army, 'Go, number
Israel, from Beer-sheba to Dan, and bring me a report, so that I may know
their number. '**3** But Joab said, 'May the Lord increase the number of his
people a hundredfold! Are they not, my lord the king, all of them my lord's
servants? Why then should my lord require this? Why should he bring guilt
on Israel? '**4** But the king's word prevailed against Joab. So Joab departed and
went throughout all Israel, and came back to Jerusalem. **5** Joab gave the total
count of the people to David. In all Israel there were one million one
hundred thousand men who drew the sword, and in Judah four hundred
and seventy thousand who drew the sword. **6** But he did not include Levi
and Benjamin in the numbering, for the king's command was abhorrent to
Joab.

7 But God was displeased with this thing, and he struck Israel. **8** David said to
God, 'I have sinned greatly in that I have done this thing. But now, I pray
you, take away the guilt of your servant; for I have done very foolishly. '**9** The
Lord spoke to Gad, David's seer, saying, **10** 'Go and say to David, "Thus says
the Lord: Three things I offer you; choose one of them, so that I may do it to
you. '"**11** So Gad came to David and said to him, 'Thus says the Lord, "Take

your choice: [12] either three years of famine; or three months of devastation by your foes, while the sword of your enemies overtakes you; or three days of the sword of the Lord, pestilence on the land, and the angel of the Lord destroying throughout all the territory of Israel." Now decide what answer I shall return to the one who sent me. '[13] Then David said to Gad, 'I am in great distress; let me fall into the hand of the Lord, for his mercy is very great; but let me not fall into human hands.'

[14] So the Lord sent a pestilence on Israel; and seventy thousand persons fell in Israel. [15] And God sent an angel to Jerusalem to destroy it; but when he was about to destroy it, the Lord took note and relented concerning the calamity; he said to the destroying angel, 'Enough! Stay your hand. 'The angel of the Lord was then standing by the threshing-floor of Ornan the Jebusite. [16] David looked up and saw the angel of the Lord standing between earth and heaven, and in his hand a drawn sword stretched out over Jerusalem. Then David and the elders, clothed in sackcloth, fell on their faces. [17] And David said to God, 'Was it not I who gave the command to count the people? It is I who have sinned and done very wickedly. But these sheep, what have they done? Let your hand, I pray, O Lord my God, be against me and against my father's house; but do not let your people be plagued!

Visio Divina

"Bonaparte Visits the Plague Stricken in Jaffa" by Antoine-Jean Gros (1804)

Poema Divina

Do Not Go Gentle" by Dylan Thomas

Do not go gentle into that good night,
Old age should burn and rave at close of day;
Rage, rage against the dying of the light.

Though wise men at their end know dark is right,
Because their words had forked no lightning they
Do not go gentle into that good night.

Good men, the last wave by, crying how bright
Their frail deeds might have danced in a green bay,
Rage, rage against the dying of the light.

Wild men who caught and sang the sun in flight,
And learn, too late, they grieved it on its way,
Do not go gentle into that good night.

Grave men, near death, who see with blinding sight

Blind eyes could blaze like meteors and be gay,

Rage, rage against the dying of the light.

And you, my father, there on the sad height,

Curse, bless, me now with your fierce tears, I pray.

Do not go gentle into that good night.

Rage, rage against the dying of the light.

Audio Divina

Your Peace Will Make Us One" by Audrey Assad

Daily Prayer:

Father God, illuminate the places that we are not in alignment with your will. Correct us in those places, and lead us on the path towards righteousness. Give us empathy for the struggle of our fellow human beings, and foster compassion and kindness in us. Amen.

TUESDAY

Lectio Divina

Psalm 17

¹ Hear a just cause, O Lord; attend to my cry;
   give ear to my prayer from lips free of deceit.

² From you let my vindication come;
   let your eyes see the right.

³ If you try my heart, if you visit me by night,
      if you test me, you will find no wickedness in me;
      my mouth does not transgress.
   ⁴ As for what others do, by the word of your lips
   I have avoided the ways of the violent.
   ⁵ My steps have held fast to your paths;
      my feet have not slipped.

⁶ I call upon you, for you will answer me, O God;
      incline your ear to me, hear my words.
   ⁷ Wondrously show your steadfast love,
      O saviour of those who seek refuge
      from their adversaries at your right hand.

⁸ Guard me as the apple of the eye;
      hide me in the shadow of your wings,
   ⁹ from the wicked who despoil me,
      my deadly enemies who surround me.
   ¹⁰ They close their hearts to pity;
      with their mouths they speak arrogantly.
   ¹¹ They track me down;[a] now they surround me;
      they set their eyes to cast me to the ground.

¹² They are like a lion eager to tear,
   like a young lion lurking in ambush.

¹³ Rise up, O Lord, confront them, overthrow them!
   By your sword deliver my life from the wicked,
   ¹⁴ from mortals—by your hand, O Lord—
   from mortals whose portion in life is in this world.
   May their bellies be filled with what you have stored up for them;
   may their children have more than enough;
   may they leave something over to their little ones.

¹⁵ As for me, I shall behold your face in righteousness;
   when I awake I shall be satisfied, beholding your likeness.

Visio Divina

"Over the Waves" by Setsuko Matsushima (2011)

Poema Divina

Let Evening Come" by Jane Kenyon

Let the light of late afternoon
shine through chinks in the barn, moving
up the bales as the sun moves down.

Let the cricket take up chafing
as a woman takes up her needles
and her yarn. Let evening come.

Let dew collect on the hoe abandoned
in long grass. Let the stars appear
and the moon disclose her silver horn.

Let the fox go back to its sandy den.
Let the wind die down. Let the shed
go black inside. Let evening come.

To the bottle in the ditch, to the scoop
in the oats, to air in the lung
let evening come.

Let it come, as it will, and don t
be afraid. God does not leave us
comfortless, so let evening come.

Audio Divina
The Wolves" by Ben Howard

Daily Prayer
Father God who is with us in the depths of our despair, help us to always be aware of Your presence. Let us be wrapped in the knowledge that You are here with us, our Guide and our Comforter, and give us peace. Amen

WEDNESDAY

**Lectio Divina**

Job 1:1-22

[1] There was once a man in the land of Uz whose name was Job. That man was blameless and upright, one who feared God and turned away from evil. [2] There were born to him seven sons and three daughters. [3] He had seven thousand sheep, three thousand camels, five hundred yoke of oxen, five hundred donkeys, and very many servants; so that this man was the greatest of all the people of the east. [4] His sons used to go and hold feasts in one another's houses in turn; and they would send and invite their three sisters to eat and drink with them. [5] And when the feast days had run their course, Job would send and sanctify them, and he would rise early in the morning and offer burnt-offerings according to the number of them all; for Job said, 'It may be that my children have sinned, and cursed God in their hearts. 'This is what Job always did.

[6] One day the heavenly beings came to present themselves before the Lord, and Satan also came among them. [7] The Lord said to Satan, 'Where have you come from? 'Satan answered the Lord, 'From going to and fro on the earth, and from walking up and down on it. '[8] The Lord said to Satan, 'Have you considered my servant Job? There is no one like him on the earth, a blameless and upright man who fears God and turns away from evil. '[9] Then Satan answered the Lord, 'Does Job fear God for nothing? [10] Have you not put a fence around him and his house and all that he has, on every side? You have blessed the work of his hands, and his possessions have increased in the land. [11] But stretch out your hand now, and touch all that he has, and he will curse you to your face. '[12] The Lord said to Satan, 'Very well, all that he has is in your power; only do not stretch out your hand against him! 'So Satan went out from the presence of the Lord.

¹³ One day when his sons and daughters were eating and drinking wine in the eldest brother's house, ¹⁴ a messenger came to Job and said, 'The oxen were ploughing and the donkeys were feeding beside them, ¹⁵ and the Sabeans fell on them and carried them off, and killed the servants with the edge of the sword; I alone have escaped to tell you. '¹⁶ While he was still speaking, another came and said, 'The fire of God fell from heaven and burned up the sheep and the servants, and consumed them; I alone have escaped to tell you. '¹⁷ While he was still speaking, another came and said, 'The Chaldeans formed three columns, made a raid on the camels and carried them off, and killed the servants with the edge of the sword; I alone have escaped to tell you. '¹⁸ While he was still speaking, another came and said, 'Your sons and daughters were eating and drinking wine in their eldest brother's house, ¹⁹ and suddenly a great wind came across the desert, struck the four corners of the house, and it fell on the young people, and they are dead; I alone have escaped to tell you.'

²⁰ Then Job arose, tore his robe, shaved his head, and fell on the ground and worshipped. ²¹ He said, 'Naked I came from my mother's womb, and naked shall I return there; the Lord gave, and the Lord has taken away; blessed be the name of the Lord.'

²² In all this Job did not sin or charge God with wrongdoing.

Visio Divina
Job and His Friends" by Ilya Repin (1869)

Poema Divina

Every Morning" by Mary Oliver

I read the papers,

I unfold them and examine them in the sunlight.

The way the red mortars, in photographs,

arc down into the neighborhoods

like stars, the way death

combs everything into a gray rubble before

the camera moves on. What

dark part of my soul

shivers: you don't want to know more

about this. And then: you don't know anything

unless you do. How the sleepers

wake and run to the cellars,

how the children scream, their tongues

trying to swim away–

how the morning itself appears

like a slow white rose

while the figures climb over the bubbled thresholds,

move among the smashed cars, the streets

where the clanging ambulances won't

stop all day–death and death, messy death–

death as history, death as a habit–

how sometimes the camera pauses while a family

counts itself, and all of them are alive,

their mouths dry caves of wordlessness

in the smudged moons of their faces,

a craziness we have so far no name for–

all this I read in the papers,

in the sunlight,

I read with my cold, sharp eyes.

Audio Divina

I Have Made Mistakes" by The Oh Hellos

Daily Prayer

Father God, let us never be blind to the injustices and sufferings of this world. Be with us in our grief, for ourselves and for others. Amen

THURSDAY

Philippians 3:2-12

[2] Beware of the dogs, beware of the evil workers, beware of those who mutilate the flesh! [3] For it is we who are the circumcision, who worship in the Spirit of God and boast in Christ Jesus and have no confidence in the flesh— [4] even though I, too, have reason for confidence in the flesh.

If anyone else has reason to be confident in the flesh, I have more: [5] circumcised on the eighth day, a member of the people of Israel, of the tribe of Benjamin, a Hebrew born of Hebrews; as to the law, a Pharisee; [6] as to zeal, a persecutor of the church; as to righteousness under the law, blameless.

[7] Yet whatever gains I had, these I have come to regard as loss because of Christ. [8] More than that, I regard everything as loss because of the surpassing value of knowing Christ Jesus my Lord. For his sake I have suffered the loss of all things, and I regard them as rubbish, in order that I may gain Christ [9] and be found in him, not having a righteousness of my own that comes from the law, but one that comes through faith in Christ, the righteousness from God based on faith. [10] I want to know Christ and the power of his resurrection and the sharing of his sufferings by becoming like him in his death, [11] if somehow I may attain the resurrection from the dead.

[12] Not that I have already obtained this or have already reached the goal; but I press on to make it my own, because Christ Jesus has made me his own.

Visio Divina
"No. 2" by Mark Rothko (1962)

Poema Divina
Perhaps the World Ends Here" by Joy Harjo

The world begins at a kitchen table. No matter what, we must eat to live.

The gifts of earth are brought and prepared, set on the table. So it has been
  since creation, and it will go on.

We chase chickens or dogs away from it. Babies teethe at the corners. They
  scrape their knees under it.

It is here that children are given instructions on what it means to be human.
  We make men at it, we make women.

At this table we gossip, recall enemies and the ghosts of lovers.

Our dreams drink coffee with us as they put their arms around our children. They laugh with us at our poor falling-down selves and as we put ourselves back together once again at the table.

This table has been a house in the rain, an umbrella in the sun.

Wars have begun and ended at this table. It is a place to hide in the shadow of terror. A place to celebrate the terrible victory.

We have given birth on this table, and have prepared our parents for burial here.

At this table we sing with joy, with sorrow. We pray of suffering and remorse. We give thanks.

Perhaps the world will end at the kitchen table, while we are laughing and crying, eating of the last sweet bite.

Audio Divina
"creature" - half*alive

Daily Prayer
Father God, we are grateful for Your sacrifice. Let us never be blind to the realization of the depths of Your love for the world and may it inform the way we, too, love the world. Amen.

FRIDAY

1 The Lord is my light and my salvation;
  whom shall I fear?
 The Lord is the stronghold[a] of my life;
  of whom shall I be afraid?

2 When evildoers assail me
  to devour my flesh—
 my adversaries and foes—
  they shall stumble and fall.

3 Though an army encamp against me,
  my heart shall not fear;
 though war rise up against me,
  yet I will be confident.

4 One thing I asked of the Lord,
  that will I seek after:
 to live in the house of the Lord
  all the days of my life,
 to behold the beauty of the Lord,
  and to inquire in his temple.

5 For he will hide me in his shelter
  in the day of trouble;
 he will conceal me under the cover of his tent;
  he will set me high on a rock.

6 Now my head is lifted up
  above my enemies all around me,
 and I will offer in his tent

sacrifices with shouts of joy;
    I will sing and make melody to the Lord.

7 Hear, O Lord, when I cry aloud,
    be gracious to me and answer me!

8 'Come, 'my heart says, 'seek his face!'
    Your face, Lord, do I seek.

9 Do not hide your face from me.
    Do not turn your servant away in anger,
        you who have been my help.
    Do not cast me off, do not forsake me,
        O God of my salvation!

10 If my father and mother forsake me,
    the Lord will take me up.

11 Teach me your way, O Lord,
    and lead me on a level path
    because of my enemies.

12 Do not give me up to the will of my adversaries,
    for false witnesses have risen against me,
    and they are breathing out violence.

13 I believe that I shall see the goodness of the Lord
    in the land of the living.

14 Wait for the Lord;
    be strong, and let your heart take courage;
    wait for the Lord!

Visio Divina

"*The Kiss*" by Gustav Klimt (1907-1908)

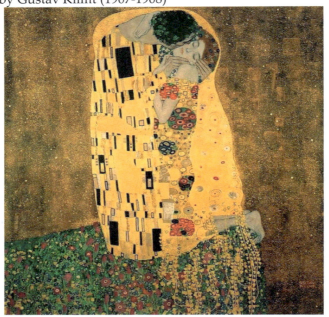

Poema Divina

"*Most Wanted*" by Mohja Kahf

Warning: God has slipped the noose.

We must confirm the worst

of our righteous fears –

God has escaped the mosque,

the synagogue, the church

where we've locked up God for years.

God is on the loose.

Henceforth beware:

You may find God in heathen beauty.

You may stumble upon God unaware.

Take appropriate measures:

You may have to behave

as if each human being
could reflect God's face.

Audio Divina
"Movements" by Rend Collective

Daily Prayer
Father God, thank You for Your constant presence and Your everlasting faithfulness. Help us to see You in all things, to know and seek to understand Your omnipotence. Amen.

SATURDAY

Lectio Divina
Psalm 118: 26-29

26 Blessed is the one who comes in the name of the Lord.[a]
  We bless you from the house of the Lord.

27 The Lord is God,
  and he has given us light.
 Bind the festal procession with branches,
  up to the horns of the altar.[b]

28 You are my God, and I will give thanks to you;
  you are my God, I will extol you.

29 O give thanks to the Lord, for he is good,
  for his steadfast love endures for ever.

Visio Divina

"*Tongues (Holy Rollers)*" by Archibald John Motley Jr. (1929)

Poema Divina:
 This Morning" by Jay Wright

This morning I threw the windows
of my room open, the light burst
in like crystal gauze and I hung
it on my wall to frame.
And here I am watching it take possession
of my room, watching the obscure love
match of light and shadow — of cold and warmth.
It is a matter of acceptance, I guess.
It is a matter of finding some room
with shadows to embrace, open. Now
the light has settled in, I don't think
I shall ever close my windows again.

Audio Divina

"*Forever*" by Chris Tomlin

Daily Prayer

Father God, give us a spirit of gratitude that can only come from You. Let us always be cognizant of the gifts and promises You have given us, and let us always be willing to praise You. Amen.

The Examen

1.   What part of this week's devotional stood out to you? How did it impact your prayers and spiritual growth?

2.   How did you handle challenges or moments of inspiration this week? Did they encourage you to take a new step in your faith?

3.   How has this week's practice helped you understand Lent and prepare for Easter? Has your view of sacrifice, repentance, or forgiveness changed?

4.   Are there any distractions or habits you'd like to let go of to make Lent more meaningful? How will you plan to create a peaceful, reflective space for yourself each day?

THE SECOND
WEEK OF LENT

SUNDAY

Lectio Divina
Luke 9:28-36

28 Now about eight days after these sayings Jesus[a] took with him Peter and John and James, and went up on the mountain to pray. 29 And while he was praying, the appearance of his face changed, and his clothes became dazzling white. 30 Suddenly they saw two men, Moses and Elijah, talking to him. 31 They appeared in glory and were speaking of his departure, which he was about to accomplish at Jerusalem. 32 Now Peter and his companions were weighed down with sleep; but since they had stayed awake,[b] they saw his glory and the two men who stood with him. 33 Just as they were leaving him, Peter said to Jesus, 'Master, it is good for us to be here; let us make three dwellings, one for you, one for Moses, and one for Elijah'—not knowing what he said. 34 While he was saying this, a cloud came and overshadowed them; and they were terrified as they entered the cloud. 35 Then from the cloud came a voice that said, 'This is my Son, my Chosen; listen to him! '36 When the voice had spoken, Jesus was found alone. And they kept silent and in those days told no one any of the things they had seen.

Visio Divina

"Icon with the Transfiguration of Jesus" by Unknown (The Russian School)

Poema Divina

Jesus on the Mountain Peak" by Brian A. Wren

Jesus, on the mountain peak,
stands alone in glory blazing.
Let us, if we dare to speak,
join the saints and angels praising:
Alleluia!

Trembling at his feet we saw
Moses and Elijah speaking.
All the Prophets and the Law
shout through them their joyful greeting:
Alleluia!

Swift the cloud of glory came,

God, proclaiming in its thunder,
Jesus as the Son by name!
Nations, cry aloud in wonder:
Alleluia!

Jesus is the chosen One,
living hope of every nation,
hear and heed him, everyone;
sing, with earth and all creation,
Alleluia!

Audio Divina
Fill My Cup" by Thad Cockrell

Daily Prayer
Father God, Living Word and shining Sun of God, in your presence we see
the face of holiness. Overshadow us with your power and grace so that we
may keep your commandments and speak your truth with courage and love.
Amen.

MONDAY

The Weekly Collect

O God, whose glory it is always to have mercy: Be gracious
to all who have gone astray from your ways, and bring them
again with penitent hearts and steadfast faith to embrace and hold fast the
unchangeable truth of your Word, Jesus Christ your Son; who with you and
the Holy Spirit lives and reigns, one God, for ever and ever. *Amen.*

Lectio Divina

Psalm 105

[1] O give thanks to the Lord, call on his name,
  make known his deeds among the peoples.
  [2] Sing to him, sing praises to him;
  tell of all his wonderful works.
  [3] Glory in his holy name;
  let the hearts of those who seek the Lord rejoice.
  [4] Seek the Lord and his strength;
  seek his presence continually.
  [5] Remember the wonderful works he has done,
  his miracles, and the judgements he has uttered,
  [6] O offspring of his servant Abraham,
  children of Jacob, his chosen ones.
  [7] He is the Lord our God;
  his judgements are in all the earth.
  [8] He is mindful of his covenant forever,
  of the word that he commanded, for a thousand generations,
  [9] the covenant that he made with Abraham,
  his sworn promise to Isaac,
  [10] which he confirmed to Jacob as a statute,
  to Israel as an everlasting covenant,
  [11] saying, 'To you I will give the land of Canaan

as your portion for an inheritance.'
¹² When they were few in number,
of little account, and strangers in it,
¹³ wandering from nation to nation,
from one kingdom to another people,
¹⁴ he allowed no one to oppress them;
he rebuked kings on their account,
¹⁵ saying, 'Do not touch my anointed ones;
do my prophets no harm.'
¹⁶ When he summoned famine against the land,
and broke every staff of bread,
¹⁷ he had sent a man ahead of them,
Joseph, who was sold as a slave.
¹⁸ His feet were hurt with fetters,
his neck was put in a collar of iron;
¹⁹ until what he had said came to pass,
the word of the Lord kept testing him.
²⁰ The king sent and released him;
the ruler of the peoples set him free.
²¹ He made him lord of his house,
and ruler of all his possessions,
²² to instruct his officials at his pleasure,
and to teach his elders wisdom.
²³ Then Israel came to Egypt;
Jacob lived as an alien in the land of Ham.
²⁴ And the Lord made his people very fruitful,
and made them stronger than their foes,
²⁵ whose hearts he then turned to hate his people,
to deal craftily with his servants.
²⁶ He sent his servant Moses,
and Aaron whom he had chosen.
²⁷ They performed his signs among them,
and miracles in the land of Ham.
²⁸ He sent darkness, and made the land dark;
they rebelled against his words.

²⁹ He turned their waters into blood,

and caused their fish to die.

³⁰ Their land swarmed with frogs,

even in the chambers of their kings.

³¹ He spoke, and there came swarms of flies,

and gnats throughout their country.

³² He gave them hail for rain,

and lightning that flashed through their land.

³³ He struck their vines and fig trees,

and shattered the trees of their country.

³⁴ He spoke, and the locusts came,

and young locusts without number;

³⁵ they devoured all the vegetation in their land,

and ate up the fruit of their ground.

³⁶ He struck down all the firstborn in their land,

the first issue of all their strength.

³⁷ Then he brought Israel out with silver and gold,

and there was no one among their tribes who stumbled.

³⁸ Egypt was glad when they departed,

for dread of them had fallen upon it.

³⁹ He spread a cloud for a covering,

and fire to give light by night.

⁴⁰ They asked, and he brought quails,

and gave them food from heaven in abundance.

⁴¹ He opened the rock, and water gushed out;

it flowed through the desert like a river.

⁴² For he remembered his holy promise,

and Abraham, his servant.

Visio Divina
"Night Blossoms" by Erin Hanson (2024)

Poema Divina
"March" by Alex Dimitrov

Every time I feel close
to understanding the world
the white kettle on my stove sounds
and I rise, attending to it
with annoyance and the pleasure
of the unmade cup of tea.
This is what it's like to live in March
or perhaps always, an unconvincing word
in any context. Blue-gold on night's branches
what part do we take in the play?
Whose turn is it to perform competence
and knowledge in the absence of both?
Unable to feel anything against the wind
I know it is spring. Time tells me so.
Never (equally as unconvincing)
have I been someone with faith in order
and human law. Love is unpredictable.
Spring arrives regardless.

Audio Divina

Is He Worthy' by Andrew Petersen

Daily Prayer

Father God, let us see You in whatever ways we worship this week. Help us hear Your voice in the places we normally think are silent, and help us think creatively about You. Amen.

TUESDAY

Lectio Divina

Numbers 14:10-24

¹⁰ But the whole congregation threatened to stone them.

Then the glory of the Lord appeared at the tent of meeting to all the Israelites. ¹¹ And the Lord said to Moses, 'How long will this people despise me? And how long will they refuse to believe in me, in spite of all the signs that I have done among them? ¹² I will strike them with pestilence and disinherit them, and I will make of you a nation greater and mightier than they.'

¹³ But Moses said to the Lord, 'Then the Egyptians will hear of it, for in your might you brought up this people from among them, ¹⁴ and they will tell the inhabitants of this land. They have heard that you, O Lord, are in the midst of this people; for you, O Lord, are seen face to face, and your cloud stands over them and you go in front of them, in a pillar of cloud by day and in a pillar of fire by night. ¹⁵ Now if you kill this people all at one time, then the nations who have heard about you will say, ¹⁶ "It is because the Lord was not able to bring this people into the land he swore to give them that he has slaughtered them in the wilderness." ¹⁷ And now, therefore, let the power of the Lord be great in the way that you promised when you spoke, saying,

¹⁸"The Lord is slow to anger,
   and abounding in steadfast love,
   forgiving iniquity and transgression,
   but by no means clearing the guilty,
   visiting the iniquity of the parents
   upon the children
   to the third and the fourth generation."

¹⁹ Forgive the iniquity of this people according to the greatness of your steadfast love, just as you have pardoned this people, from Egypt even until now.'

²⁰ Then the Lord said, 'I do forgive, just as you have asked; ²¹ nevertheless— as I live, and as all the earth shall be filled with the glory of the Lord— ²² none of the people who have seen my glory and the signs that I did in Egypt and in the wilderness, and yet have tested me these ten times and have not obeyed my voice, ²³ shall see the land that I swore to give to their ancestors; none of those who despised me shall see it. ²⁴ But my servant Caleb, because he has a different spirit and has followed me wholeheartedly, I will bring into the land into which he went, and his descendants shall possess it.

"*The Sun, 1909*" by Edvard Munch (1911)

Poema Divina

God Says Yes To Me" by Kaitlyn Haught

I asked God if it was okay to be melodramatic

and she said yes

I asked her if it was okay to be short

and she said it sure is

I asked her if I could wear nail polish

or not wear nail polish

and she said honey

she calls me that sometimes

she said you can do just exactly

what you want to

Thanks God I said

And is it even okay if I don't paragraph

my letters

Sweetcakes God said

who knows where she picked that up

what I'm telling you is

Yes Yes Yes

Audio Divina

Bad Blood" by Sleeping At Last

Daily Prayer

Father God, we are reminded that prayer is a powerful weapon and we do not take the invitation to speak directly to you lightly. Thank you for your nearness and that you gather us into conversation with you. Amen.

WEDNESDAY

Lectio Divina
Luke 13:22-31

22 Then Jesus went through the towns and villages, teaching as he made his way to Jerusalem. 23 Someone asked him, "Lord, are only a few people going to be saved?"

He said to them, 24 "Make every effort to enter through the narrow door, because many, I tell you, will try to enter and will not be able to. 25 Once the owner of the house gets up and closes the door, you will stand outside knocking and pleading, 'Sir, open the door for us.'

"But he will answer, 'I don't know you or where you come from.'

26 "Then you will say, 'We ate and drank with you, and you taught in our streets.'

27 "But he will reply, 'I don't know you or where you come from. Away from me, all you evildoers!'

28 "There will be weeping there, and gnashing of teeth, when you see Abraham, Isaac and Jacob and all the prophets in the kingdom of God, but you yourselves thrown out. 29 People will come from east and west and north and south, and will take their places at the feast in the kingdom of God. 30 Indeed there are those who are last who will be first, and first who will be last."

31 At that time some Pharisees came to Jesus and said to him, "Leave this place and go somewhere else. Herod wants to kill you."

Visio Divina

"*Blau de Colors- El Tubo*" by Montserrat Cadell Blasco (2019

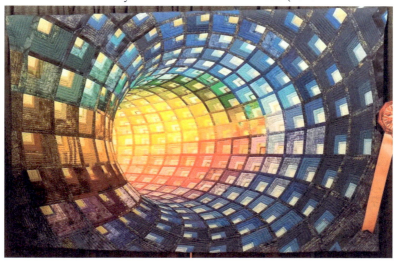

Poema Divina

Have You Ever Tried to Enter the Long Black Branches" by Mary Oliver

Have you ever tried to enter the long black branches of other lives --
tried to imagine what the crisp fringes, full of honey, hanging
from the branches of the young locust trees, in early morning, feel like?

Do you think this world was only an entertainment for you?

Never to enter the sea and notice how the water divides
with perfect courtesy, to let you in!

Never to lie down on the grass, as though you were the grass!
Never to leap to the air as you open your wings over the dark acorn of your
heart!

No wonder we hear, in your mournful voice, the complaint
that something is missing from your life!

Who can open the door who does not reach for the latch?
Who can travel the miles who does not put one foot
in front of the other, all attentive to what presents itself
continually?

Who will behold the inner chamber who has not observed
with admiration, even with rapture, the outer stone?

Well, there is time left --
fields everywhere invite you into them.

And who will care, who will chide you if you wander away
from wherever you are, to look for your soul?

Quickly, then, get up, put on your coat, leave your desk!

To put one's foot into the door of the grass, which is
the mystery, which is death as well as life, and
not be afraid!

To set one's foot in the door of death, and be overcome
with amazement!

To sit down in front of the weeds, and imagine
god the ten-fingered, sailing out of his house of straw,
nodding this way and that way, to the flowers of the
present hour, to the song falling out of the mockingbird's pink mouth,
to the tippets of the honeysuckle, that have openedin the night

To sit down, like a weed among weeds, and rustle in the wind!

Listen, are you breathing just a little, and calling it a life?

While the soul, after all, is only a window,
and the opening of the window no more difficult

than the wakening from a little sleep.

Only last week I went out among the thorns and said
to the wild roses:
deny me not,
    but suffer my devotion.
Then, all afternoon, I sat among them. Maybe

I even heard a curl or two of music, damp and rouge red,
hurrying from their stubby buds, from their delicate watery bodies.

For how long will you continue to listen to those dark shouters,
caution and prudence?
Fall in! Fall in!

A woman standing in the weeds.
A small boat flounders in the deep waves, and what's coming next
is coming with its own heave and grace.

Meanwhile, once in a while, I have chanced, among the quick things,
upon the immutable.
What more could one ask?

And I would touch the faces of the daises,
and I would bow down
to think about it.

That was then, which hasn't ended yet.

Now the sun begins to swing down. Under the peach-light,
I cross the fields and the dunes, I follow the ocean's edge.

I climb, I backtrack.
I float.
I ramble my way home.

Audio Divina
"Home II" by Dotan

Daily Prayer
Father God, in our humanness, we often forget to see the image of God in others. In our comings and goings this week, help us to see your face in everyone we interact with, giving us compassion and love for our fellow children of God. Amen.

THURSDAY

Daniel 3:19-30

[19] Then Nebuchadnezzar was furious with Shadrach, Meshach and Abednego, and his attitude toward them changed. He ordered the furnace heated seven times hotter than usual [20] and commanded some of the strongest soldiers in his army to tie up Shadrach, Meshach and Abednego and throw them into the blazing furnace. [21] So these men, wearing their robes, trousers, turbans and other clothes, were bound and thrown into the blazing furnace. [22] The king's command was so urgent and the furnace so hot that the flames of the fire killed the soldiers who took up Shadrach, Meshach and Abednego,[23] and these three men, firmly tied, fell into the blazing furnace.

[24] Then King Nebuchadnezzar leaped to his feet in amazement and asked his advisers, "Weren't there three men that we tied up and threw into the fire?"

They replied, "Certainly, Your Majesty."

[25] He said, "Look! I see four men walking around in the fire, unbound and unharmed, and the fourth looks like a son of the gods."

[26] Nebuchadnezzar then approached the opening of the blazing furnace and shouted, "Shadrach, Meshach and Abednego, servants of the Most High God, come out! Come here!"

So Shadrach, Meshach and Abednego came out of the fire, [27] and the satraps, prefects, governors and royal advisers crowded around them. They saw that the fire had not harmed their bodies, nor was a hair of their heads singed; their robes were not scorched, and there was no smell of fire on them.

28 Then Nebuchadnezzar said, "Praise be to the God of Shadrach, Meshach and Abednego, who has sent his angel and rescued his servants! They trusted in him and defied the king's command and were willing to give up their lives rather than serve or worship any god except their own God. 29 Therefore I decree that the people of any nation or language who say anything against the God of Shadrach, Meshach and Abednego be cut into pieces and their houses be turned into piles of rubble, for no other god can save in this way."

30 Then the king promoted Shadrach, Meshach and Abednego in the province of Babylon.

Visio Divina

"In the Fiery Furnace" by Chris Cook (Unknown)

Poema Divina

The Thing Is" by Ellen Bass

The Thing Is…
to love life, to love it even
when you have no stomach for it
and everything you've held dear
crumbles like burnt paper in your hands,
your throat filled with the silt of it.
When grief sits with you, its tropical heat
thickening the air, heavy as water
more fit for gills than lungs;
when grief weights you like your own flesh
only more of it, an obesity of grief,
you think, How can a body withstand this?
Then you hold life like a face
between your palms, a plain face,

no charming smile, no violet eyes,
and you say, yes, I will take you
I will love you, again.

Audio Divina
"*Mindful*" by Tow'rs

Daily Prayer
Father God, in the midst of our hardest moments, you are present with us. You do not let us go through this world alone, and we thank you for that. Help us to endure what needs to be endured, and restore our soul. Amen.

FRIDAY

Lectio Divina
Revelation 3:1-6

To the angel of the church in Sardis write:

These are the words of him who holds the seven spirits of God and the seven stars. I know your deeds; you have a reputation of being alive, but you are dead. ² Wake up! Strengthen what remains and is about to die, for I have found your deeds unfinished in the sight of my God. ³ Remember, therefore, what you have received and heard; hold it fast, and repent. But if you do not wake up, I will come like a thief, and you will not know at what time I will come to you.

⁴ Yet you have a few people in Sardis who have not soiled their clothes. They will walk with me, dressed in white, for they are worthy. ⁵ The one who is victorious will, like them, be dressed in white. I will never blot out the name of that person from the book of life, but will acknowledge that name before my Father and his angels. ⁶ Whoever has ears, let them hear what the Spirit says to the churches.

Visio Divina

*"Incensing the Veil "*by John Singer Sargent (1880)

Poema Divina

Meditations in an Emergency" by Cameron Awkward-Rich

I wake up & it breaks my heart. I draw the blinds &
the thrill of rain breaks my heart. I go outside. I
ride the train, walk among the buildings, men in
Monday suits. The flight of doves, the city of tents
beneath the underpass, the huddled mass, old
women hawking roses, & children all of them,
break my heart. There's a dream I have in which I

love the world. I run from end to end like fingers
through her hair. There are no borders, only wind.
Like you, I was born. Like you, I was raised in the
 institution of dreaming. Hand on my heart. Hand
on my stupid heart.

Audio Divina
"_Skeleton Bones_" by John Mark McMillan

Daily Prayer
Father God, wake us up to the work that needs to be done around us. Help
us be people after your own heart, participating in the creation and
recreation that is the Kingdom breaking in. Amen

SATURDAY

Lectio Divina
Luke 6:43-45

[43] "No good tree bears bad fruit, nor does a bad tree bear good fruit. [44] Each tree is recognized by its own fruit. People do not pick figs from thornbushes, or grapes from briers. [45] A good man brings good things out of the good stored up in his heart, and an evil man brings evil things out of the evil stored up in his heart. For the mouth speaks what the heart is full of.

Visio Divina
"The Four Trees" by Claude Monet (1891)

Poema Divina

Small Kindnesses" by Danusha Laméris

I've been thinking about the way, when you walk
down a crowded aisle, people pull in their legs
to let you by. Or how strangers still say "bless you"
when someone sneezes, a leftover
from the Bubonic plague. "Don't die," we are saying.
And sometimes, when you spill lemons
from your grocery bag, someone else will help you
pick them up. Mostly, we don't want to harm each other.
We want to be handed our cup of coffee hot,
and to say thank you to the person handing it. To smile
at them and for them to smile back. For the waitress
to call us honey when she sets down the bowl of clam chowder,
and for the driver in the red pick-up truck to let us pass.
We have so little of each other, now. So far
from tribe and fire. Only these brief moments of exchange.
What if they are the true dwelling of the holy, these
fleeting temples we make together when we say, "Here,
have my seat," "Go ahead—you first," "I like your hat."

Audio Divina

Oslo" by De Joie

Daily Prayer

Father God, let our actions be evidence of your work inside of us. Let us emulate the Fruits of the Spirit, and be representatives of Jesus. Amen.

The Examen

1. What part of this week's devotional stood out to you? How did it impact your prayers and spiritual growth?
2. How did you handle challenges or moments of inspiration this week? Did they encourage you to take a new step in your faith?

3. How has this week's practice helped you understand Lent and prepare for Easter? Has your view of sacrifice, repentance, or forgiveness changed?

4. Are there any distractions or habits you'd like to let go of to make Lent more meaningful? How will you plan to create a peaceful, reflective space for yourself each day?

THE THIRD WEEK
OF LENT

SUNDAY

Lectio Divina
Psalm 63:1-8

1 You, God, are my God,
　　earnestly I seek you;
　I thirst for you,
　　my whole being longs for you,
　in a dry and parched land
　　where there is no water.
2 I have seen you in the sanctuary
　　and beheld your power and your glory.
3 Because your love is better than life,
　　my lips will glorify you.
4 I will praise you as long as I live,
　　and in your name I will lift up my hands.
5 I will be fully satisfied as with the richest of foods;
　　with singing lips my mouth will praise you.
6 On my bed I remember you;
　　I think of you through the watches of the night.
7 Because you are my help,
　　I sing in the shadow of your wings.
8 I cling to you;
　　your right hand upholds me.

Visio Divina

"*16 / 30*" by Madeleine Jubilee Saito (2022)

Poema Divina

The Orange" by Wendy Cope

At lunchtime I bought a huge orange -
The size of it made us all laugh.
I peeled it and shared it with Robert and Dave -
They got quarters and I had a half

And that orange, it made me so happy,
As ordinary things often do
Just lately. The shopping. A walk in the park.
This is peace and contentment. It's new.

The rest of the day was quite easy.
I did all the jobs on my list
And enjoyed them and had some time over.
I love you. I'm glad I exist.

Audio Divina

Belly of the Deepest Love" by Tow'rs

Daily Prayer

Father God, as we reflect on this week, let us become aware of the places where you were working, work we didn't even know was being done. Help us to be aware of your grace in the week that comes, attuned to your will and work. Amen.

MONDAY

The Weekly Collect

Almighty God, you know that we have no power in ourselves
to help ourselves: Keep us both outwardly in our bodies and
inwardly in our souls, that we may be defended from all
adversities which may happen to the body, and from all evil
thoughts which may assault and hurt the soul; through Jesus
Christ our Lord, who lives and reigns with you and the Holy
Spirit, one God, for ever and ever. Amen.

Lectio Divina
Psalm 39

¹ I said, 'I will guard my ways
   that I may not sin with my tongue;
I will keep a muzzle on my mouth
   as long as the wicked are in my presence.'
² I was silent and still;
   I held my peace to no avail;
   my distress grew worse,
³ my heart became hot within me.
While I mused, the fire burned;
   then I spoke with my tongue:
⁴' Lord, let me know my end,
   and what is the measure of my days;
   let me know how fleeting my life is.
⁵ You have made my days a few handbreadths,
   and my lifetime is as nothing in your sight.
Surely everyone stands as a mere breath.
⁶ Surely everyone goes about like a shadow.
Surely for nothing they are in turmoil;
   they heap up, and do not know who will gather.

⁷‘ And now, O Lord, what do I wait for?
    My hope is in you.
⁸ Deliver me from all my transgressions.
    Do not make me the scorn of the fool.
⁹ I am silent; I do not open my mouth,
    for it is you who have done it.
¹⁰ Remove your stroke from me;
    I am worn down by the blows of your hand.
¹¹‘ You chastise mortals
    in punishment for sin,
consuming like a moth what is dear to them;
    surely everyone is a mere breath.
¹²‘ Hear my prayer, O Lord,
    and give ear to my cry;
    do not hold your peace at my tears.
For I am your passing guest,
    an alien, like all my forebears.
¹³ Turn your gaze away from me, that I may smile again,
    before I depart and am no more.’

Visio Divina
"Her wisdom" by Nevena Bentz (2020)

Poema Divina
"The Shell is breaking" by Malcom Guite

Deliver me and raise me from the dead
For I have walked in shadows. Nothingness,
The vanity of things fills me with dread,

The sheer inanity, the pointlessness
Of how we used to live – we can't go back
To that – the rush that masked our emptiness,

All the pretence that covered what we lack
When what we really lacked was always you.
I held my tongue, but I could see the crack

In everything we build and say and do.
And now the crack is widening. I pray

That we will turn and see a light break through

These fissures that so fill us with dismay.
The death we fear is birth, the shell is breaking:
The stone itself will soon be rolled away.

Audio Divina
 "Create in me a Clean Heart" by Keith Green

Daily Prayer
Father we often recognize how brief and fragile our lives are on this earth.
Teach us to treasure each day, to speak only words that uplift others. Guide
and strengthen us as we walk with you. We surrender our worries and
ambitions knowing that all we have and all we are belongs to you. Guard us
from chasing fleeting pursuits, and instead, fix our hearts on your perfect
will. Lord, our hope is in you alone—help us to live in humility and faith,
honoring you in all we do. Amen.

TUESDAY

Lectio Divina
Psalm 40:5-10

⁵ You have multiplied, O Lord my God,
　your wondrous deeds and your thoughts towards us;
　none can compare with you.
Were I to proclaim and tell of them,
　they would be more than can be counted.
⁶ Sacrifice and offering you do not desire,
　but you have given me an open ear.
Burnt-offering and sin-offering
　you have not required.
⁷ Then I said, 'Here I am;
　in the scroll of the book it is written of me.
⁸ I delight to do your will, O my God;
　your law is within my heart.'
⁹ I have told the glad news of deliverance
　in the great congregation;
see, I have not restrained my lips,
　as you know, O Lord.
¹⁰ I have not hidden your saving help within my heart,
　I have spoken of your faithfulness and your salvation;
I have not concealed your steadfast love and your faithfulness
　from the great congregation.

Visio Divina
"*Psalm 40:5*" by Bible Art (2014)

Poema Divina
"*Many, O LORD my God are the Wonders you Have Done Psalm 40:5*" by Roxanne Lea Dubarry

Many, O LORD my God are the wonders you have done.

The things you have planned for us

no one can recount to you;

were I to speak and tell

of them,

they would be too many to declare.

The heavens declare the glory

of God;

the skies proclaim the work

of his hands.

O LORD, our LORD,

how majestic is your name in all

of the earth!
You have set your glory
above the heavens.

I will praise you, O LORD, with all
my heart;
I will tell of your wonders,
I will be glad and rejoice in you;
I will sing praise to your name,
O Most High.

Praise the LORD.
How good is it to sing praises to our
God,
how pleasant and fitting to praise
him!

Great is our LORD and mighty in
power;
his understanding has no limit.
The LORD sustains the humble
but casts the wicked to the
ground.

Sing to the LORD with thanksgiving;
make music to our God on the
harp.

He covers the sky with clouds;
he supplies the earth with rain
and makes grass grow on the
hills.

The LORD is my shepherd, I shall
not be in want.

He makes me to lie down in green
pastures,
he leads me besides quit waters,
he restores my soul.

Audio Divina
"God of Wonders" by Third Day

Daily Prayer
Lord, your wonders are too many to count, and your love surrounds us.
Thank you for your faithfulness and grace. Help us to proclaim your
goodness and share Your salvation boldly. May our lives reflect your truth
and love, drawing others to know you. Amen.

Lectio Divina
Luke 13:18-21

[18] He said therefore, 'What is the kingdom of God like? And to what should I compare it? [19] It is like a mustard seed that someone took and sowed in the garden; it grew and became a tree, and the birds of the air made nests in its branches.'

[20] And again he said, 'To what should I compare the kingdom of God? [21] It is like yeast that a woman took and mixed in with three measures of flour until all of it was leavened.'

Visio Divina
"The Mustard Seed" by Juliet Venter (2016)

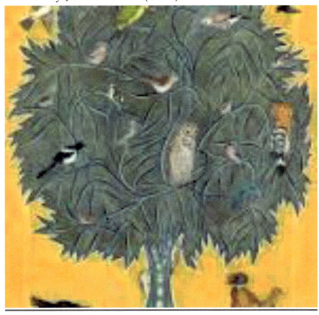

"Mustard Seed Faith" by Cat Hodgson

Transform me that I believe
You'll take care of every need

If I just have the faith
The size of a mustard seed

After all you are the one
Who on water walked

You're the only one
That could make a donkey talk

You opened eyes with mud
For someone that was blind

For a man that was mad
You sent the madness into swine

Why surely I can believe
You'll take care of every need

Help me have the faith
In your loving plan

Even though sometimes it's hard
For this mere moral to understand

Audio Divina
"Faith Of A Mustard Seed" by WorshipMob

Daily Prayer

Father, like the mustard seed that becomes a mighty tree and the yeast that transforms the dough, we bring our smallness in faith to you, asking that You grow it and deepen our trust in you. Let our hearts be fertile soil for your word, and may our actions, though they may seem small, spread your love and truth to those around us. Empower us to be part of your transforming work in the world, trusting that your kingdom will flourish in ways beyond our imagination. Amen.

THURSDAY

Lectio Divina
Psalm 32

[1] Happy are those whose transgression is forgiven,
    whose sin is covered.
[2] Happy are those to whom the Lord imputes no iniquity,
    and in whose spirit there is no deceit.
[3] While I kept silence, my body wasted away
    through my groaning all day long.
[4] For day and night your hand was heavy upon me;
    my strength was dried up as by the heat of summer.
[5] Then I acknowledged my sin to you,
    and I did not hide my iniquity;
I said, 'I will confess my transgressions to the Lord',
    and you forgave the guilt of my sin.
[6] Therefore let all who are faithful
    offer prayer to you;
at a time of distress, the rush of mighty waters
    shall not reach them.
[7] You are a hiding-place for me;
    you preserve me from trouble;
    you surround me with glad cries of deliverance.
[8] I will instruct you and teach you the way you should go;
    I will counsel you with my eye upon you.
[9] Do not be like a horse or a mule, without understanding,
    whose temper must be curbed with bit and bridle,
    else it will not stay near you.
[10] Many are the torments of the wicked,
    but steadfast love surrounds those who trust in the Lord.
[11] Be glad in the Lord and rejoice, O righteous,
    and shout for joy, all you upright in heart.

Visio Divina
"The Prodigal Son" by Clark Kelley Price (1997)

Poema Divina
"O for a Thousand Tongues to Sing" by Charles Wesley

1 O for a thousand tongues to sing
my great Redeemer's praise,
the glories of my God and King,
the triumphs of his grace!

2 My gracious Master and my God,
assist me to proclaim,
to spread thro' all the earth abroad
the honors of your name.

3 Jesus! the name that charms our fears,
that bids our sorrows cease,
'tis music in the sinner's ears,
'tis life and health and peace.

4 He breaks the power of cancelled sin,
he sets the prisoner free;
his blood can make the foulest clean;
his blood availed for me.

5 To God all glory, praise, and love

be now and ever given
by saints below and saints above,
the Church in earth and heaven.

Audio Divina
"Call Upon The Lord" by Elevation Worship

Daily Prayer
Father, we praise you for the forgiveness you have given us in Jesus Christ.
You have cast our sins as far as the east is from the west; they are gone, never
to be counted against us again. Hallelujah! Thank you for being our refuge
and for surrounding us with your steadfast love. Guide us in the way we
should go and preserve us from trouble. help us to walk in your light and
truth always. Amen.

FRIDAY

2 Cor. 5:6-15

[6] So we are always confident; even though we know that while we are at home in the body we are away from the Lord— [7] for we walk by faith, not by sight. [8] Yes, we do have confidence, and we would rather be away from the body and at home with the Lord. [9] So whether we are at home or away, we make it our aim to please him. [10] For all of us must appear before the judgement seat of Christ, so that each may receive recompense for what has been done in the body, whether good or evil.

[11] Therefore, knowing the fear of the Lord, we try to persuade others; but we ourselves are well known to God, and I hope that we are also well known to your consciences. [12] We are not commending ourselves to you again, but giving you an opportunity to boast about us, so that you may be able to answer those who boast in outward appearance and not in the heart. [13] For if we are beside ourselves, it is for God; if we are in our right mind, it is for you. [14] For the love of Christ urges us on, because we are convinced that one has died for all; therefore all have died. [15] And he died for all, so that those who live might live no longer for themselves, but for him who died and was raised for them.

<u>*Visio Divina.*</u>

"Forgiveness" by Charlie Mackesy

<u>*Poema Divina*</u>

"We walk by Faith, Not by Sight" by Deborah Ann Belka

I walk by faith,

not by sight

because Jesus

is my light.

His Word my path,

illuminates

so His step

I can duplicate.

His Spirit dwells,
inside of me
so I can trust
what I can't see.
His guidance helps,
me finally find
peace for both
heart and mind.
I walk by faith,
in His light
for I trust Jesus . . .
for my sight!

Audio Divina
"*Walk By Faith*" by Jeremy Camp

Daily Prayer
Father, walking by is hard. Guide each of our steps as you lead us into things we cannot see. Help us to live each day with purpose, knowing that one day we will stand before You. May our lives point others to you, encouraging them to walk with you as well. Fill us with your love, and help us to live in a way that honors you. May our lives reflect your grace. Amen.

SATURDAY

Lectio Divina

Luke 15:1-7

15 Now all the tax-collectors and sinners were coming near to listen to him. ² And the Pharisees and the scribes were grumbling and saying, 'This fellow welcomes sinners and eats with them.'

³ So he told them this parable: ⁴ 'Which one of you, having a hundred sheep and losing one of them, does not leave the ninety-nine in the wilderness and go after the one that is lost until he finds it? ⁵ When he has found it, he lays it on his shoulders and rejoices. ⁶ And when he comes home, he calls together his friends and neighbours, saying to them, "Rejoice with me, for I have found my sheep that was lost." ⁷ Just so, I tell you, there will be more joy in heaven over one sinner who repents than over ninety-nine righteous people who need no repentance.

⁸ 'Or what woman having ten silver coins, if she loses one of them, does not light a lamp, sweep the house, and search carefully until she finds it? ⁹ When she has found it, she calls together her friends and neighbors, saying, "Rejoice with me, for I have found the coin that I had lost." ¹⁰ Just so, I tell you, there is joy in the presence of the angels of God over one sinner who repents.'

"Jesus Bringing a Lost Lamb Home" by Melanie Pyke

Poema Divina

"The Ninety and Nine" by Elizabeth Cecilia Clephane

There were ninety and nine that safely lay
In the shelter of the fold;
But one was out on the hills away,
Far off from the gates of gold,
Away on the mountains wild and bare,
Away from the tender Shepherd's care.

"Lord, Thou hast here Thy ninety and nine—
Are they not enough for Thee?"
But the Shepherd made answer, "This of Mine
Has wandered away from Me;

And although the road be rough and steep
I go to the desert to find My sheep."

But none of the ransomed ever knew
How deep were the waters crossed;
Nor how dark was the night that the Lord passed through
Ere He found His sheep that was lost.
Out in the desert He heard its cry,
Sick and helpless and ready to die.

"Lord, whence are those blood drops all the way
That mark out the mountain's track?"
"They were shed for one who had gone astray,
Ere the Shepherd could bring him back."
"Lord, whence are Thy hands so rent and torn?"
"They were pierced tonight by many a thorn."

And all through the mountains, thunder-riven,
And up from the rocky steep,
There arose a cry to the gate of heaven,
"Rejoice, I have found My sheep!"
And the angels echoed around the throne,
"Rejoice, for the Lord brings back His own."

Audio Divina
"Reckless Love" by Corey Asbury

Daily Prayer
Father, thank you for the recklessness of your love that cares for the one who is lost. All of us have gone astray and you have gone after us to bring us back to you. Your love for us is so deep that You rejoice over our return, no matter how far we have strayed. How amazing—thank You!. We pray now for our friends and loved ones who are far from you. We pray for their return to you as well. May we always remember that your love is pursuing, drawing us all close to you. Thank you, amen.

The Examen

1. What part of this week's devotional stood out to you? How did it impact your prayers and spiritual growth?

2. How did you handle challenges or moments of inspiration this week? Did they encourage you to take a new step in your faith?

3. How has this week's practice helped you understand Lent and prepare for Easter? Has your view of sacrifice, repentance, or forgiveness changed?

4. Are there any distractions or habits you'd like to let go of to make Lent more meaningful? How will you plan to create a peaceful, reflective space for yourself each day?

THE FOURTH
WEEK OF LENT

SUNDAY

Lectio Divina
2 Corinthians 5:16-21

[16] From now on, therefore, we regard no one from a human point of view; even though we once knew Christ from a human point of view, we know him no longer in that way. [17] So if anyone is in Christ, there is a new creation: everything old has passed away; see, everything has become new! [18] All this is from God, who reconciled us to himself through Christ, and has given us the ministry of reconciliation; [19] that is, in Christ God was reconciling the world to himself, not counting their trespasses against them, and entrusting the message of reconciliation to us. [20] So we are ambassadors for Christ, since God is making his appeal through us; we entreat you on behalf of Christ, be reconciled to God. [21] For our sake he made him to be sin who knew no sin, so that in him we might become the righteousness of God.

Visio Divina
"New Creation in Christ" by PropheticVessel (2021)

Poema Divina
"Love Divine, All Love Excelling" by Charles Wesley

1 Love Divine, all love excelling,
Joy of heav'n, to earth come down;
Fix in us Thy humble dwelling,
All Thy faithful mercies crown.
Jesus, Thou art all compassion;
Pure, unbounded love Thou art;
Visit us with Thy salvation,
Enter every trembling heart.

2 Breathe, O breathe Thy loving Spirit
Into every troubled breast;

Let us all in Thee inherit,
Let us find the promised rest.
Take away the love of sinning;
Alpha and Omega be;
End of faith, as its beginning,
Set our hearts at liberty.

3 Come, Almighty, to deliver,
Let us all Thy life receive;
May Thy presence e'er be with us,
Never more Thy temples leave.
Thee we would be always blessing,
Serve Thee as Thou wouldst approve,
Pray, and praise Thee without ceasing,
Glory in Thy perfect love.

4 Finish, then, Thy new creation;
Pure and spotless let us be;
Let us see Thy great salvation
Perfectly restored in Thee;
Changed from glory into glory
Till with Thee we take our place,
Till we cast our crowns before Thee,
Lost in wonder, love and praise.

Audio Divina
"Born Again" by Third Day

Daily Prayer
Father, we thank you for reconciling us to yourself through Christ and making us new creations. Help us, as Paul teaches, to see others through your eyes and not by the world s standards. May we be faithful ambassadors of your grace, speaking and acting as ministers of reconciliation, sharing the hope and forgiveness we have received in Jesus. Let our lives reflect the peace and love that you offer to the world, and may we bear witness to the

transforming power of your grace. Lead us to live out this calling, glorifying you in all we do. Amen.

MONDAY

The Weekly Collect

Gracious Father, whose blessed Son Jesus Christ came down
from heaven to be the true bread which gives life to the world:
Evermore give us this bread, that he may live in us, and we in
him; who lives and reigns with you and the Holy Spirit, one
God, now and for ever. Amen.

Lectio Divina
Psalm 53

[1] Fools say in their hearts, 'There is no God.'
    They are corrupt, they commit abominable acts;
    there is no one who does good.
[2] God looks down from heaven on humankind
    to see if there are any who are wise,
    who seek after God.
[3] They have all fallen away, they are all alike perverse;
    there is no one who does good,
    no, not one.
[4] Have they no knowledge, those evildoers,
    who eat up my people as they eat bread,
    and do not call upon God?
[5] There they shall be in great terror,
    in terror such as has not been.
For God will scatter the bones of the ungodly;
    they will be put to shame, for God has rejected them.
[6] O that deliverance for Israel would come from Zion!
    When God restores the fortunes of his people,
    Jacob will rejoice; Israel will be glad.

Visio Divina
"*Stańczyk*" by Jan Matejko (1862)

Poema Divina
"*Psalm 53*" by Walterrean Salley

Give me the strength
To praise you Lord,
The breath to laud Your name.
You alone are glorious;
You deserve the fame.
May your kingdom ever stand
And your praises ring.
Live forever—true and grand—
Great and mighty King.

Audio Divina
"*Psalm 53*" by Poor Bishop Hooper

Daily Prayer
Father, we come to you acknowledging our need for your mercy and grace, without you, we are lost and broken. Forgive us for the times we have acted foolishly, turning from your truth or failing to seek you wholeheartedly. Remind us daily of your presence and help us to walk in humility, relying on

your wisdom rather than our own understanding. We pray for hearts that seek after you, and we long for the day when you fully restore your people. May we rejoice in Your salvation and be strengthened to live faithfully in a world that often denies you. Amen.

Lectio Divina
Leviticus 25:1-19

25 The Lord spoke to Moses on Mount Sinai, saying: ² Speak to the people of Israel and say to them: When you enter the land that I am giving you, the land shall observe a sabbath for the Lord. ³ For six years you shall sow your field, and for six years you shall prune your vineyard, and gather in their yield; ⁴ but in the seventh year there shall be a sabbath of complete rest for the land, a sabbath for the Lord: you shall not sow your field or prune your vineyard. ⁵ You shall not reap the aftergrowth of your harvest or gather the grapes of your unpruned vine: it shall be a year of complete rest for the land. ⁶ You may eat what the land yields during its sabbath—you, your male and female slaves, your hired and your bound labourers who live with you; ⁷ for your livestock also, and for the wild animals in your land all its yield shall be for food.

⁸ You shall count off seven weeks of years, seven times seven years, so that the period of seven weeks of years gives forty-nine years. ⁹ Then you shall have the trumpet sounded loud; on the tenth day of the seventh month—on the day of atonement—you shall have the trumpet sounded throughout all your land. ¹⁰ And you shall hallow the fiftieth year and you shall proclaim liberty throughout the land to all its inhabitants. It shall be a jubilee for you: you shall return, every one of you, to your property and every one of you to your family. ¹¹ That fiftieth year shall be a jubilee for you: you shall not sow, or reap the aftergrowth, or harvest the unpruned vines. ¹² For it is a jubilee; it shall be holy to you: you shall eat only what the field itself produces.

¹³ In this year of jubilee you shall return, every one of you, to your property. ¹⁴ When you make a sale to your neighbour or buy from your neighbour, you shall not cheat one another. ¹⁵ When you buy from your neighbour, you shall pay only for the number of years since the jubilee; the seller shall charge you only for the remaining crop-years. ¹⁶ If the years are more, you shall increase

the price, and if the years are fewer, you shall diminish the price; for it is a certain number of harvests that are being sold to you. [17] You shall not cheat one another, but you shall fear your God; for I am the Lord your God.

[18] You shall observe my statutes and faithfully keep my ordinances, so that you may live on the land securely. [19] The land will yield its fruit, and you will eat your fill and live on it securely.

Visio Divina
"Jubilee" by Rickie Jenkins Focus (2018)

Poema Divina
"Sabbatical" by Matthew Holloway

a time taken
to breathe
undetermined
re-evaluate the world
take stock of thoughts
and reassess them
allow the soul to rest
the heart to sleep
and the mind to be free
time has it own value

time is limitless
and it will be taken
to breathe

Audio Divina
"Days of Elijah" by Robin Mark

Daily Prayer
Father, we thank you for the lessons of jubilee and sabbath in Leviticus,
reminding us that all things belong to you and that we are called to live with
generosity and trust. Help us to embrace your vision of rest and renewal,
releasing burdens and forgiving debts, just as you forgive us. May we
remember that you are our provider, guiding us to care for one another with
compassion. Teach us to live in the freedom of holy love and justice,
reflecting your heart of mercy in all we do. Help us to trust that as we walk
in obedience, you will faithfully provide and pour out Your blessings upon
us. Amen.

WEDNESDAY

Lectio Divina
Luke 9:10-17

[10] On their return the apostles told Jesus[a] all they had done. He took them with him and withdrew privately to a city called Bethsaida. [11] When the crowds found out about it, they followed him; and he welcomed them, and spoke to them about the kingdom of God, and healed those who needed to be cured.

[12] The day was drawing to a close, and the twelve came to him and said, 'Send the crowd away, so that they may go into the surrounding villages and countryside, to lodge and get provisions; for we are here in a deserted place. '[13] But he said to them, 'You give them something to eat. 'They said, 'We have no more than five loaves and two fish—unless we are to go and buy food for all these people. '[14] For there were about five thousand men. And he said to his disciples, 'Make them sit down in groups of about fifty each. '[15] They did so and made them all sit down. [16] And taking the five loaves and the two fish, he looked up to heaven, and blessed and broke them, and gave them to the disciples to set before the crowd. [17] And all ate and were filled. What was left over was gathered up, twelve baskets of broken pieces.

"Icon of the Feeding of the 5000" by Fr. William (Bill) K. Foss (2011)

Poema Divina
"5 Loaves Of Bread And 2 Fish" by Randy L. McClave

There stood hungry five thousand men

And their wives and children also stood with them,

They stood and heard the lord's preaching

Then they followed the lord's teaching.

Then when the Lord had finished his sermon

Their choices the congregation had to determine,

Then they all said no to sin

Then unto the Lord they all said, 'Amen! '

The followers of the Lord were now all hungry

Growling of their stomachs that were all now empty,

The disciples didn't know what they could do

The disciples were worried not having a clue.

How could they send those thousands away

As they were now all starving on that day,

They all needed food/ something to eat

But, they had no money for meat.

The disciples then went up to their most Holy Pastor

Their most caring and loving Pastor,

They asked the Lord how can we feed such a large crowd

In such a desolate place were emptiness is allowed.

The disciples didn't know how the Multitude would be fed

Then Andrew brought a boy who had some fish and bread,

As though the lord Jesus had granted a wish

The Lord fed everyone with five loaves of bread and two fish.

Audio Divina
"Five Loaves and Two Fishes" by Corrinn May

Daily Prayer
Father, thank you for the compassion and power you displayed in feeding
the five thousand. You took what seemed small and insignificant, blessed it,
and made it more than enough. Teach us to place our small resources in your
hands, trusting that you can make them sufficient for any need. Help us to
see those around us through your eyes of compassion and to serve with
generous hearts. Remind us that you are the source of all provision and are
all-sufficient for every need we face. Thank you, Father. Amen.

THURSDAY

¹ But now thus says the Lord,
   he who created you, O Jacob,
   he who formed you, O Israel:
Do not fear, for I have redeemed you;
   I have called you by name, you are mine.
² When you pass through the waters, I will be with you;
   and through the rivers, they shall not overwhelm you;
when you walk through fire you shall not be burned,
   and the flame shall not consume you.
³ For I am the Lord your God,
   the Holy One of Israel, your Saviour.
I give Egypt as your ransom,
   Ethiopia and Seba in exchange for you.
⁴ Because you are precious in my sight,
   and honoured, and I love you,
I give people in return for you,
   nations in exchange for your life.
⁵ Do not fear, for I am with you;
   I will bring your offspring from the east,
   and from the west I will gather you;
⁶ I will say to the north, 'Give them up',
   and to the south, 'Do not withhold;
bring my sons from far away
   and my daughters from the end of the earth—
⁷ everyone who is called by my name,
   whom I created for my glory,
   whom I formed and made.'

Visio Divina
"King of Glory" by Yongsung Kim (2015)

Poema Divina
"I am not Alone" by Babatunde Aremu

I know I am not alone
There is a witness in my heart
His manifest presence are obvious
His hosts are around me
Teleguiding every move I made
He is always there with me

When I stumbles
He bears me up
I am hemed before and behind
By his cords of defence
He is my impregnable fortress
That never break ranks

He is always with me
He perceives my thought

He knows my desires
He lightens my dark paths
And prevents me from blindness
He knows me in and out

My creator is my companion
My steps are teleguided by him
Before my words are uttered
He knows and answers ahead
His banal over me is awesome
What a marvellous companion!

My wisdom, knowledge, prosperity
Joy, peace, health and uncountable blessings
Are generously donated from his throne
What will I render to Him
He is just too marvellous
His companionship is incomprehensible

Audio Divina
"I Am Not Alone" by Kari Jobe

Daily Prayer
Father, thank you for the promise that you have called us by name and that we are yours. In times of fear and uncertainty, help us to remember that you are always with us, guiding and protecting us. Remind us of our worth in your eyes and fill our hearts with peace, knowing that you love us deeply. Strengthen our faith as we face life's challenges, and help us to trust in your unwavering presence and provision. May we live boldly, reflecting your love to those around us. Amen.

FRIDAY

Lectio Divina
Psalm 126

[1] When the Lord restored the fortunes of Zion,
   we were like those who dream.
[2] Then our mouth was filled with laughter,
   and our tongue with shouts of joy;
then it was said among the nations,
   'The Lord has done great things for them.'
[3] The Lord has done great things for us,
   and we rejoiced.
[4] Restore our fortunes, O Lord,
   like the watercourses in the Negeb.
[5] May those who sow in tears
   reap with shouts of joy.
[6] Those who go out weeping,
   bearing the seed for sowing,
shall come home with shouts of joy,
   carrying their sheaves.

Visio Divina
"Filled with Joy" by OverflowArtStudio (2020)

Poema Divina
"O For a Thousand Tongues to Sing" by Charles Wesley

1 O for a thousand tongues to sing
  My great Redeemer's praise,
The glories of my God and King,
  The triumphs of His grace.

2 My gracious Master and my God,
  Assist me to proclaim,
To spread through all the earth abroad,
  The honors of Thy name.

3 Jesus! the name that charms our fears,
  That bids our sorrows cease;
'Tis music in the sinner's ears,

'Tis life, and health, and peace.

4 His love my heart has captive made,
  His captive would I be,
For He was bound, and scourged and died,
  My captive soul to free.

5 He breaks the power of canceled sin,
  He sets the prisoner free;
His blood can make the foulest clean;
  His blood availed for me.

6 So now Thy blessed Name I love,
  Thy will would e'er be mine.
Had I a thousand hearts to give,
  My Lord, they all were Thine!

Audio Divina
"Psalm 126" (featuring Paul Zach and Jessica Fox) by the Porter's Gate

Daily Prayer
Father, we thank you for the joy that overflows when you restore us, just as you did for Israel. When we look back at what you have done, we remember that you turn our tears into laughter and our weeping into songs of joy. We ask for that same spirit of renewal today. Restore our hearts and refresh our lives like streams in the desert, bringing life and fruitfulness where there was barrenness. May our lives be a testimony of your faithfulness, and may we carry your joy as we sow in hope, trusting that you will bring a harvest of gladness in your perfect time. Amen.

SATURDAY

Lectio Divina
Exodus 12:21-27

²¹ Then Moses called all the elders of Israel and said to them, 'Go, select lambs for your families, and slaughter the passover lamb. ²² Take a bunch of hyssop, dip it in the blood that is in the basin, and touch the lintel and the two doorposts with the blood in the basin. None of you shall go outside the door of your house until morning. ²³ For the Lord will pass through to strike down the Egyptians; when he sees the blood on the lintel and on the two doorposts, the Lord will pass over that door and will not allow the destroyer to enter your houses to strike you down. ²⁴ You shall observe this rite as a perpetual ordinance for you and your children. ²⁵ When you come to the land that the Lord will give you, as he has promised, you shall keep this observance. ²⁶ And when your children ask you, "What do you mean by this observance?" ²⁷ you shall say, "It is the passover sacrifice to the Lord, for he passed over the houses of the Israelites in Egypt, when he struck down the Egyptians but spared our houses. "'And the people bowed down and worshipped.

"The Passover Instituted" by Thomas Henry (1859)

Poema Divina

"Today... 'Christ Our Passover Lamb' " by Roy Allen

'I'll pass over you when I see the blood'
This was the wonderful promise of God
The blood has been shed and the price is paid
The Passover Lamb on the alter laid.

The day was the day of Unleavened Bread
The day that the Passover Lamb lay dead
Christ our Passover Lamb has now been slain
And His blood has cleansed us from sins stain.

From His lips I have heard 'Father forgive'
And because He has died I now shall live
The judgement of God has been waived for me
Because of what Jesus did at Calvary.

Audio Divina
"Passover Lamb" by Matthew Adams

Daily Prayer
Father, we thank you for the powerful reminder of your protection and
deliverance shown in the Passover. Just as you sheltered the Israelites under
the blood of the lamb, we trust in your saving grace over our lives today.
Help us to remember your bold and mighty acts, as we reflect on how you
have brought us from darkness to light. May we never take your protection
for granted, and may our gratitude deepen with each remembrance of your
faithfulness. Teach us to share this story of salvation with those around us,
so that all may know your love and find refuge in you. Amen.

The Examen
1.   What part of this week's devotional stood out to you? How did it
     impact your prayers and spiritual growth?
2.   How did you handle challenges or moments of inspiration this week?
     Did they encourage you to take a new step in your faith?
3.   How has this week's practice helped you understand Lent and prepare
     for Easter? Has your view of sacrifice, repentance, or forgiveness
     changed?
4.   Are there any distractions or habits you'd like to let go of to make Lent
     more meaningful? How will you plan to create a peaceful, reflective
     space for yourself each day?

THE FIFTH WEEK OF LENT

SUNDAY

Lectio Divina
Psalm 145

1   I will extol you, my God and King,
        and bless your name forever and ever.
2   Every day I will bless you,
        and praise your name forever and ever.
3   Great is the Lord, and greatly to be praised;
        his greatness is unsearchable.

4   One generation shall laud your works to another,
        and shall declare your mighty acts.
5   On the glorious splendor of your majesty,
        and on your wondrous works, I will meditate.
6   The might of your awesome deeds shall be proclaimed,
        and I will declare your greatness.
7   They shall celebrate the fame of your abundant goodness,
        and shall sing aloud of your righteousness.

8   The Lord is gracious and merciful,
        slow to anger and abounding in steadfast love.
9   The Lord is good to all,
        and his compassion is over all that he has made.

10   All your works shall give thanks to you, O Lord,
        and all your faithful shall bless you.
11   They shall speak of the glory of your kingdom,
        and tell of your power,
12   to make known to all people your mighty deeds,
        and the glorious splendor of your kingdom.
13   Your kingdom is an everlasting kingdom,
        and your dominion endures throughout all generations.

    The Lord is faithful in all his words,
        and gracious in all his deeds.
14   The Lord upholds all who are falling,

122

and raises up all who are bowed down.

15   The eyes of all look to you,
        and you give them their food in due season.

16   You open your hand,
        satisfying the desire of every living thing.

17   The Lord is just in all his ways,
        and kind in all his doings.

18   The Lord is near to all who call on him,
        to all who call on him in truth.

19   He fulfills the desire of all who fear him;
        he also hears their cry, and saves them.

20   The Lord watches over all who love him,
        but all the wicked he will destroy.

21   My mouth will speak the praise of the Lord,
        and all flesh will bless his holy name forever and ever.

Visio Divina

"Those Who Sow in Tears Shall Reap in Joy" by Deborah Nell (2016)

"Those Who Sow in Tears" by Frank McEleny

The rains that fall from Heaven
Fall down upon our face
And the dawn is surely coming
Yet in the darkness we embrace

Perhaps you've never seen the dawn
Yet in your heart you know its true
That beyond the edge of all you know
There is a sky that's ever blue

To plough the field of perpetual winter
For a harvest never seen before
Is to walk in darkness without stumbling
Is to open up the heavenly door

What lies beyond, no one can see
Yet through the door there is no fears
This is a place where seeds are found
They are for those who sow in tears

And with the seeds and with our tears
We'll plough the fields until the end
With weeping hearts the seeds are watered
And then the harvest God will send

Then all our tears are wiped away
Our hearts are filled with laughter
We now embrace perpetual dawn
And blue skies ever after!

Audio Divina
"Great Things" by Phil Wickham

Daily Prayer

Father, we rejoice in your power to restore and renew. When we feel lost or weary, remind us of the joy you bring, like streams in the desert. Turn our tears into laughter and our waiting into a harvest of hope. We lift up those who are in a season of sadness and mourning; pour out your comfort and grace upon them. May our lives reflect the goodness of your love as we trust in Your promises, both now and always. Amen.

MONDAY

The Weekly Collect

Almighty and everliving God, in your tender love for the human race you sent your Son our Savior Jesus Christ to take upon him our nature, and to suffer death upon the cross, giving us the example of his great humility: Mercifully grant that we may walk in the way of his suffering, and also share in his resurrection; through Jesus Christ our Lord, who lives and reigns with you and the Holy Spirit, one God, for ever and ever. Amen.

Lectio Divina
Hebrews 10:19-25

19 Therefore, my friends, since we have confidence to enter the sanctuary by the blood of Jesus, 20 by the new and living way that he opened for us through the curtain (that is, through his flesh), 21 and since we have a great priest over the house of God, 22 let us approach with a true heart in full assurance of faith, with our hearts sprinkled clean from an evil conscience and our bodies washed with pure water. 23 Let us hold fast to the confession of our hope without wavering, for he who has promised is faithful. 24 And let us consider how to provoke one another to love and good deeds, 25 not neglecting to meet together, as is the habit of some, but encouraging one another, and all the more as you see the Day approaching.

"Hold Fast" by Andrew Forrest (2017)

Poema Divina

"Hold Fast" by Carmela Patterson

Perseverance is a virtue great blessings to imbue
Through it the soul is nurtured as it heeds every cue
From the Holy Spirit who indwells within it if it is true
To the faith of our fathers who guides us through
This earthly life on our way to heaven above
Where finally we'll rest in God's peace and love.

Hold fast!

While the road we travel is strewn with rocks and hills
And we are faced with pain, suffering and many ills,
Still we hold to the faith we were taught
Even though with slings and arrows we are fraught
Sliding and hiding, caught in the tangle
of satan trying every angle
our souls to wrangle.

Hold fast!

He comes, the Lord God of Hosts
The liar-satan snidely boasts
And sneakily slips away,
No more to hold us sway.
Our Savior bathes us in His Blood
His Graces our souls to flood

Hold fast!

HE COMES!

Audio Divina
"He Will Hold Me Fast" by Keith & Kristyn Getty

Daily Prayer
Father, thank you for the work of Jesus Christ, which gives us the confidence to approach you. In these days, help us to draw nearer to you with holy hearts. Strengthen us to hold fast to the hope we have in you, and guide us to encourage one another in our walk with you. Shape us into a community that reflects your holy love and transforming power. Amen.

TUESDAY

Lectio Divina
Psalm 20

1 The Lord answer you in the day of trouble!
  The name of the God of Jacob protect you!
2 May he send you help from the sanctuary,
  and give you support from Zion.
3 May he remember all your offerings,
  and regard with favor your burnt sacrifices.
4 May he grant you your heart's desire,
  and fulfill all your plans.
5 May we shout for joy over your victory,
  and in the name of our God set up our banners.
May the Lord fulfill all your petitions.
6 Now I know that the Lord will help his anointed;
  he will answer him from his holy heaven
  with mighty victories by his right hand.
7 Some take pride in chariots, and some in horses,
  but our pride is in the name of the Lord our God.
8 They will collapse and fall,
  but we shall rise and stand upright.
9 Give victory to the king, O Lord;
  answer us when we call.

<u>*Visio Divina*</u>

"Chariot with Four Horses" marble bas-relief from the ancient agora of Athens.
(4th century BCE)

<u>*Poema Divina*</u>

"Psalm 20" by Isaac Watts

Prayer and hope of victory.
For a day of prayer in time of war.

Now may the God of power and grace
Attend his people's humble cry!
Jehovah hears when Isr'el prays,
And brings deliverance from on high.

The name of Jacob's God defends
Better than shields or brazen walls;
He from his sanctuary sends
Succor and strength, when Zion calls.

Well he remembers all our sighs,
His love exceeds our best deserts;
His love accepts the sacrifice
Of humble groans and broken hearts.

In his salvation is our hope,
And, in the name of Isr'el's God,
Our troops shall lift their banners up,
Our navies spread their flags abroad.

Some trust in horses trained for war,
And some of chariots make their boasts:
Our surest expectations are
From thee, the Lord of heav'nly hosts.

[O may the memory of thy name
Inspire our armies for the fight!
Our foes shall fall and die with shame,
Or quit the field with shameful flight.]

Now save us, Lord, from slavish fear,
Now let our hopes be firm and strong,
Till the salvation shall appear,
And joy and triumph raise the song.

Audio Divina
"*Psalm 20*" by Shane and Shane

Daily Prayer
Father, we come before you today with the assurance that you are our help
in times of trouble and that you are our strength in weakness. Thank you for
walking with us through every trial we face. May we never forget that our
strength comes from you. May our lives bring you glory as we trust you each
step of the way. Amen.

WEDNESDAY

Lectio Divina
Habakkuk 3:2-15

2 O Lord, I have heard of your renown,
  and I stand in awe, O Lord, of your work.
In our own time revive it;
  in our own time make it known;
  in wrath may you remember mercy.
3 God came from Teman,
  the Holy One from Mount Paran.
His glory covered the heavens,
  and the earth was full of his praise.
4 The brightness was like the sun;
  rays came forth from his hand,
  where his power lay hidden.
5 Before him went pestilence,
  and plague followed close behind.
6 He stopped and shook the earth;
  he looked and made the nations tremble.
The eternal mountains were shattered;
  along his ancient pathways
  the everlasting hills sank low.
7 I saw the tents of Cushan under affliction;
  the tent-curtains of the land of Midian trembled.
8 Was your wrath against the rivers O Lord?
  Or your anger against the rivers,
  or your rage against the sea,
when you drove your horses,
  your chariots to victory?
9 You brandished your naked bow,
  sated were the arrows at your command
  You split the earth with rivers.

¹⁰ The mountains saw you, and writhed;
　a torrent of water swept by;
the deep gave forth its voice.
　The sun raised high its hands;
¹¹ the moon stood still in its exalted place,
　at the light of your arrows speeding by,
　at the gleam of your flashing spear.
¹² In fury you trod the earth,
　in anger you trampled nations.
¹³ You came forth to save your people,
　to save your anointed.
You crushed the head of the wicked house,
　laying it bare from foundation to roof.
¹⁴ You pierced with their own arrows the head of his warriors,
　who came like a whirlwind to scatter us,
　gloating as if ready to devour the poor who were in hiding.
¹⁵ You trampled the sea with your horses,
　churning the mighty waters.

Visio Divina
"Habakkuk 3:3" by Bible Art (2014)

Poema Divina
"This Awesome God" by Michael P. Johnson

Whose eyes behold the might of seas
Who hear a mountain stream
Surveying tall majestic trees
Can see it's not a dream

Can see creation at a glance
Life's jewel box unsealed
Without great pomp or circumstance
God's mighty hand revealed

This awesome God still much unknown
So little taken heed
Looks ever from His Glory Throne

To meet our daily need

This righteous God who sees all things
The secrets each would hide
Who hears each song creation sings
Who knows our thoughts inside

This self same God is deep in love
This God so few exalt
Enthroned majestically above
Is jealous to a fault

He knows our names our every flaw
Each evil we connive
Yet choice blessings He longs to pour
To help the lost survive

This God of ours loves you and I
Although the grave awaits
Unwilling we as sinners die
He opened wide His gates

He sent His son to die instead
To save who've gone astray
To heal our souls give daily bread
Until the youngest day

Audio Divina
"Indescribable" by Chris Tomlin

Daily Prayer
Father, we stand in awe of your power displayed through the ages. Revive your work
among us in our time, we pray. Though we face trials and uncertainty, help us
remember the mighty acts you have performed and trust in your goodness and
unfailing love. We rest in You, our refuge and strength. Amen.

THURSDAY

Lectio Divina
Psalm 31:9-16

⁹ Be gracious to me, O Lord, for I am in distress;
    my eye wastes away from grief,
    my soul and body also.
¹⁰ For my life is spent with sorrow,
    and my years with sighing;
my strength fails because of my misery,
    and my bones waste away.
¹¹ I am the scorn of all my adversaries,
    a horror to my neighbors,
an object of dread to my acquaintances;
    those who see me in the street flee from me.
¹² I have passed out of mind like one who is dead;
    I have become like a broken vessel.
¹³ For I hear the whispering of many—
    terror all around!—
as they scheme together against me,
    as they plot to take my life.
¹⁴ But I trust in you, O Lord;
    I say, 'You are my God.'
¹⁵ My times are in your hand;
    deliver me from the hand of my enemies and persecutors.
¹⁶ Let your face shine upon your servant;
    save me in your steadfast love.

Visio Divina

"Self Portrait (in Distress)" by Edvard Munch (1919)

Poema Divina

"God is Our Refuge in Distress" by Martin Luther

God is our refuge in distress,
Our shield of hope through every care,
Our Shepherd watching us to bless,
And therefore will we not despair;
Although the mountains shake,
And hills their place forsake,
And billows o'er them break
Yet still will we not fear,
For Thou, O God, art ever near.

God is our hope and strength in woe;

Through earth He maketh wars to cease;

His power breaketh spear and bow;

His mercy sendeth endless peace.

Then though the earth remove,

And storms rage high above,

And seas tempestuous prove,

Yet still will we not fear,

The Lord of Hosts is ever near.

Audio Divina
"Lord, I Need You" by Matt Maher

Daily Prayer
Father, we come before you in our weakness, burdened at times by sorrow and overwhelmed by life's struggles. you see the anguish in our hearts and every silent tear. In our distress, we seek refuge in you, our rock and fortress. Hear our cries and grant us the strength to endure. Remind us of your constant love and faithfulness in moments of despair. Teach us to love and support one another as you have loved us, and let your light shine through our lives to bring hope to those who feel lost. May your presence bring us peace, and may we honor you in all we do. Amen.

FRIDEY

Lectio Divina
Hebrews 2:10-18

[10] It was fitting that God, for whom and through whom all things exist, in bringing many children to glory, should make the pioneer of their salvation perfect through sufferings. [11] For the one who sanctifies and those who are sanctified all have one Father. For this reason Jesus is not ashamed to call them brothers and sisters, [12] saying,
'I will proclaim your name to my brothers and sisters,
   in the midst of the congregation I will praise you.'
[13] And again,

'I will put my trust in him.'
And again,

'Here am I and the children whom God has given me.'
[14] Since, therefore, the children share flesh and blood, he himself likewise shared the same things, so that through death he might destroy the one who has the power of death, that is, the devil, [15] and free those who all their lives were held in slavery by the fear of death. [16] For it is clear that he did not come to help angels, but the descendants of Abraham. [17] Therefore he had to become like his brothers and sisters in every respect, so that he might be a merciful and faithful high priest in the service of God, to make a sacrifice of atonement for the sins of the people. [18] Because he himself was tested by what he suffered, he is able to help those who are being tested.

Visio Divina

"I am Among You as One Who Serves" by Ben and Catherine Taylor (2019)

Poema Divina

"And Can it Be" by Charles Wesley

1. And can it be that I should gain
   An int'rest in the Savior's blood?
   Died He for me, who caused His pain—
   For me, who Him to death pursued?
   Amazing love! How can it be,
   That Thou, my God, shouldst die for me?
   - *Refrain:*
     Amazing love! How can it be,
     That Thou, my God, shouldst die for me?

2. 'Tis myst'ry all: th 'Immortal dies:
   Who can explore His strange design?
   In vain the firstborn seraph tries
   To sound the depths of love divine.
   Tis mercy all! Let earth adore,
   Let angel minds inquire no more.

3. He left His Father's throne above—
   So free, so infinite His grace—
   Emptied Himself of all but love,
   And bled for Adam's helpless race:
   Tis mercy all, immense and free,
   For, O my God, it found out me!

4. Long my imprisoned spirit lay,
   Fast bound in sin and nature's night;
   Thine eye diffused a quick'ning ray—
   I woke, the dungeon flamed with light;
   My chains fell off, my heart was free,
   I rose, went forth, and followed Thee.

5. No condemnation now I dread;
   Jesus, and all in Him, is mine;
   Alive in Him, my living Head,
   And clothed in righteousness divine,
   Bold I approach th 'eternal throne,
   And claim the crown, through Christ my own.

Audio Divina
"Man of Sorrows" by Hillsong Worship

Daily Prayer
Father, we stand in awe of your humility and love. You sent your son Jesus, to take on our humanity and share in our struggles. He faced hunger, thirst, suffering, temptation, and even death to bring us life. Thank you for his willingness to become like us, to endure what we endure, and to destroy the power of sin and death over us. He truly is our faithful High Priest, who understands our weaknesses and stands ready to help us in every trial. Strengthen us, Father, to follow his example. Amen.

SATURDAY

Lectio Divina
Luke 22:1-13

¹ Now the festival of Unleavened Bread, which is called the Passover, was near. ² The chief priests and the scribes were looking for a way to put Jesus to death, for they were afraid of the people.

³ Then Satan entered into Judas called Iscariot, who was one of the twelve; ⁴ he went away and conferred with the chief priests and officers of the temple police about how he might betray him to them. ⁵ They were greatly pleased and agreed to give him money. ⁶ So he consented and began to look for an opportunity to betray him to them when no crowd was present.

⁷ Then came the day of Unleavened Bread, on which the Passover lamb had to be sacrificed. ⁸ So Jesus sent Peter and John, saying, 'Go and prepare the Passover meal for us that we may eat it. '⁹ They asked him, 'Where do you want us to make preparations for it? '¹⁰ 'Listen, 'he said to them, 'when you have entered the city, a man carrying a jar of water will meet you; follow him into the house he enters ¹¹ and say to the owner of the house, "The teacher asks you, 'Where is the guest room, where I may eat the Passover with my disciples?'" ¹² He will show you a large room upstairs, already furnished. Make preparations for us there. '¹³ So they went and found everything as he had told them; and they prepared the Passover meal.

Visio Divina

A painting of a Jewish Seder (cropped) by Mathilde Hahn Meyerin (1861-1936)

Poema Divina

"The Last Supper" by Linda Kruschke

The hour was late

His time was near

Emmanuel would be a sacrifice dear

Lamb for the Passover

All the disciples partake

Soon a new covenant

The Savior would make

Setting the table in the

Upper room for the feast

Prepared in advance His last

Passover meal; He broke bread without yeast

E'er you eat the bread and drink the wine

Remember Him, who for you became least

Audio Divina

"The Passover Song" by Caroline Cobb

Daily Prayer

Father, preparation is important. Just as Jesus instructed his disciples to make preparation for the Passover meal, may we also prepare our hearts to commune with you in a deeper way this season. Help us to be ready to serve in whatever ways you ask. Help us to honor your presence in our lives each day, drawing closer to you in all we do. Amen.

The Examen

1. What part of this week's devotional stood out to you? How did it impact your prayers and spiritual growth?
2. How did you handle challenges or moments of inspiration this week? Did they encourage you to take a new step in your faith?
3. How has this week's practice helped you understand Lent and prepare for Easter? Has your view of sacrifice, repentance, or forgiveness changed?
4. Are there any distractions or habits you'd like to let go of to make Lent more meaningful? How will you plan to create a peaceful, reflective space for yourself each day?

HOLY WEEK

PALM SUNDAY

Luke 19:28-40

28 After he had said this, he went on ahead, going up to Jerusalem. 29 When he had come near Bethphage and Bethany, at the place called the Mount of Olives, he sent two of the disciples, 30 saying, "Go into the village ahead of you, and as you enter it you will find tied there a colt that has never been ridden. Untie it and bring it here. 31 If anyone asks you, 'Why are you untying it?' just say this, 'The Lord needs it.' " '32 So those who were sent departed and found it as he had told them. 33 As they were untying the colt, its owners asked them, "Why are you untying the colt?" 34 They said, "The Lord needs it." 35 Then they brought it to Jesus; and after throwing their cloaks on the colt, they set Jesus on it. 36 As he rode along, people kept spreading their cloaks on the road. 37 As he was now approaching the path down from the Mount of Olives, the whole multitude of the disciples began to praise God joyfully with a loud voice for all the deeds of power that they had seen, 38 saying,

> "Blessed is the king
>   who comes in the name of the Lord!
> Peace in heaven,
>   and glory in the highest heaven!"

39 Some of the Pharisees in the crowd said to him, "Teacher, order your disciples to stop." 40 He answered, "I tell you, if these were silent, the stones would shout out."

Visio Divina

"Christ's Triumphal Entry into Jerusalem" by Félix Louis Leullier (1820)

Poema Divina

"Hosanna, Loud Hosanna" by William Monk

Hosanna, loud hosanna,
    The little children sang;
    Through pillared court and temple
    The lovely anthem rang.
    To Jesus, who had blessed them
    Close folded to His breast,
    The children sang their praises,
    The simplest and the best.

From Olivet they followed
    Mid an exultant crowd,
    The victor palm branch waving,
    And chanting clear and loud;
    Bright angels joined the chorus,
    Beyond the cloudless sky,
      Hosanna in the highest,
    Glory to God on high!"

Fair leaves of silvery olive
> They strewed upon the ground,
> While Salem's circling mountains
> Echoed the joyful sound;
> The Lord of men and angels
> Rode on in lowly state,
> Nor scorned that little children
> Should on His bidding wait.

"Hosanna in the highest!"
> That ancient song we sing,
> For Christ is our Redeemer,
> The Lord of Heaven our king.
> O may we ever praise Him
> With heart and life and voice,
> And in His blissful presence
> Eternally rejoice!

Audio Divina
"Blessed Is He Who Comes" by Paul Wilbur

Daily Prayer
Hosanna! Blessed is he who comes in the name of the Lord! Father, we join our voices with the joyful shouts of the crowd that welcomed Jesus on his way into Jerusalem. We rejoice to welcome him as our King, even as we remember that He entered the holy city to fulfill your deeper purpose. He came not to receive praise, but to bear the cross for the sin of the world. And so once more, we cry, "Hosanna! Blessed is he who comes in the name of the Lord!" Amen.

HOLY MONDAY

The Weekly Collect

Almighty God, whose dear Son went not up to joy but
first he suffered pain, and entered not into glory before he
was crucified: Mercifully grant that we, walking in the way
of the cross, may find it none other that the way of life and
peace; through Jesus Christ your Son our Lord, who lives
and reigns with you and the Holy Spirit, one God, for ever
and ever. Amen.

Lectio Divina
John 12:1-11

Six days before the Passover Jesus came to Bethany, the home of Lazarus,
whom he had raised from the dead. [2] There they gave a dinner for him.
Martha served, and Lazarus was one of those at the table with him. [3] Mary
took a pound of costly perfume made of pure nard, anointed Jesus 'feet, and
wiped them with her hair. The house was filled with the fragrance of the
perfume. [4] But Judas Iscariot, one of his disciples (the one who was about to
betray him), said, [5] "Why was this perfume not sold for three hundred denarii
and the money given to the poor?" [6] (He said this not because he cared about
the poor, but because he was a thief; he kept the common purse and used to
steal what was put into it.) [7] Jesus said, "Leave her alone. She bought it so that
she might keep it for the day of my burial. [8] You always have the poor with
you, but you do not always have me."

[9] When the great crowd of the Jews learned that he was there, they came not
only because of Jesus but also to see Lazarus, whom he had raised from the
dead. [10] So the chief priests planned to put Lazarus to death as well, [11] since it
was on account of him that many of the Jews were deserting and were
believing in Jesus.

Visio Divina
"*Come to Bethany*" by Heather Choate Davis (2016)

Poema Divina
"*Broken and Spilled Out*" by Bill and Gloria Gaither

One day a plain village woman

Driven by love for her Lord

Recklessly poured out a valuable essence

Disregarding the scorn

And once it was broken and spilled out

A fragrance filled all the room

Like a prisoner released from his shackles

Like a spirit set free from the tomb

[Chorus]

Broken and spilled out
Just for love of you, Jesus
My most precious treasure
Lavished on thee
Broken and spilled out
And poured at your feet
In sweet abandon
Let me be spilled out
And used up for Thee

[Verse 2]
Lord, You were God's precious treasure
His love and His own perfect Son
Sent here to show me the love of the Father
Just for love, it was done
And though You were perfect and holy
You gave up yourself willingly
You spared no expense for my pardon
You were used up and wasted for me

[Chorus]
Broken and spilled out
Just for love of me, Jesus
God's most precious treasure
Lavished on me
Broken and spilled out
And poured at my feet
In sweet abandon
Lord, you were spilled out
And used up for me

[Outro]
In sweet abandon
Lord, you were spilled out
And used up for me

<u>*Audio Divina*</u>
"Alabaster Box" by CeCe Winans

<u>*Daily Prayer*</u>
Father, thank you for the beautiful display of love that Mary poured out at the feet of Jesus. Help us to follow her example, giving of ourselves as freely as she did in our service to you and others. Transform our hearts so that our worship becomes not just an action, but a way of life. May we glorify you in every act of love we share, and may our lives reflect the depth of our devotion to you. Amen.

HOLY TUESDAY

Lectio Divina
John 12:20-36

[20] Now among those who went up to worship at the festival were some Greeks. [21] They came to Philip, who was from Bethsaida in Galilee, and said to him, "Sir, we wish to see Jesus." [22] Philip went and told Andrew; then Andrew and Philip went and told Jesus. [23] Jesus answered them, "The hour has come for the Son of Man to be glorified. [24] Very truly, I tell you, unless a grain of wheat falls into the earth and dies, it remains just a single grain; but if it dies, it bears much fruit. [25] Those who love their life lose it, and those who hate their life in this world will keep it for eternal life. [26] Whoever serves me must follow me, and where I am, there will my servant be also. Whoever serves me, the Father will honor.

[27] "Now my soul is troubled. And what should I say—'Father, save me from this hour'? No, it is for this reason that I have come to this hour. [28] Father, glorify your name." Then a voice came from heaven, "I have glorified it, and I will glorify it again." [29] The crowd standing there heard it and said that it was thunder. Others said, "An angel has spoken to him." [30] Jesus answered, "This voice has come for your sake, not for mine. [31] Now is the judgment of this world; now the ruler of this world will be driven out. [32] And I, when I am lifted up from the earth, will draw all people to myself." [33] He said this to indicate the kind of death he was to die. [34] The crowd answered him, "We have heard from the law that the Messiah remains forever. How can you say that the Son of Man must be lifted up? Who is this Son of Man?" [35] Jesus said to them, "The light is with you for a little longer. Walk while you have the light, so that the darkness may not overtake you. If you walk in the darkness, you do not know where you are going. [36] While you have the light, believe in the light, so that you may become children of light." After Jesus had said this, he departed and hid from them.

Visio Divina
"John 12:24" by Bible Art (2014)

Poema Divina
"Today... 'The Grain Of Wheat' " by Roy Allen

The grain of wheat that fell into the ground and died
was none other than Jesus Christ the crucified.
He gave His life a sacrifice so that we might live
and as He died out loud He cried "Father forgive."
Now from the travail of His soul He can now see
multitudes that have been saved for eternity.

Audio Divina
"When a Grain of Wheat Falls" by Sarah Begaj

Daily Prayer
Father, thank you for the powerful lesson of the grain of wheat—that
through death, new life emerges. Through Jesus' death, we now have new,
abundant, and eternal life. Thank you, Lord. Help us release the things in our
lives that need to die so that new life can take root. Transform us into new

creations, and grant us the courage to embrace change as you mold us into who you desire us to be. May we continually grow deeper in faith, bearing fruit that honors you. Amen.

HOLY WEDNESDAY

Lectio Divina
John 13:21-32

21 After saying this Jesus was troubled in spirit, and declared, "Very truly, I tell you, one of you will betray me." 22 The disciples looked at one another, uncertain of whom he was speaking. 23 One of his disciples—the one whom Jesus loved—was reclining next to him; 24 Simon Peter therefore motioned to him to ask Jesus of whom he was speaking. 25 So while reclining next to Jesus, he asked him, "Lord, who is it?" 26 Jesus answered, "It is the one to whom I give this piece of bread when I have dipped it in the dish." So when he had dipped the piece of bread, he gave it to Judas son of Simon Iscariot. 27 After he received the piece of bread, Satan entered into him. Jesus said to him, "Do quickly what you are going to do." 28 Now no one at the table knew why he said this to him. 29 Some thought that, because Judas had the common purse, Jesus was telling him, "Buy what we need for the festival"; or, that he should give something to the poor. 30 So, after receiving the piece of bread, he immediately went out. And it was night. 31 When he had gone out, Jesus said, "Now the Son of Man has been glorified, and God has been glorified in him. 32 If God has been glorified in him, God will also glorify him in himself and will glorify him at once.

"The Last Supper; Christ Washing the Apostles' Feet" Unknown (c.1400–10)

Poema Divina

"The Feet of Judas" by George Marion McClellan

Christ washed the feet of Judas!
The dark and evil passions of his soul,
His secret plot, and sordidness complete,
His hate, his purposing, Christ knew the whole,
And still in love he stooped and washed his feet.

Christ washed the feet of Judas!
Yet all his lurking sin was bare to him,
His bargain with the priest, and more than this,
In Olivet, beneath the moonlight dim,
Aforehand knew and felt his treacherous kiss.

Christ washed the feet of Judas!
And so ineffable his love 'twas meet,
That pity fill his great forgiving heart,
And tenderly to wash the traitor's feet,
Who in his Lord had basely sold his part.

Christ washed the feet of Judas!
And thus a girded servant, self-abased,
Taught that no wrong this side the gate of heaven
Was ever too great to wholly be effaced,
And though unasked, in spirit be forgiven.

And so if we have ever felt the wrong
Of trampled rights, of caste, it matters not,
What e'er the soul has felt or suffered long,
Oh, heart! this one thing should not be forgot:
Christ washed the feet of Judas.

Audio Divina
"Jesus is Betrayed by Judas // The Golgotha Experience" by Poor Bishop Hooper

Daily Prayer
Father, we remember the intense pain of betrayal that Jesus experienced from someone who had followed him closely for three years. Thank you for his example of grace and love, even in the face of such hurt. You call us to love our enemies and pray for those who persecute us, and to turn the other cheek when we are struck. Help us to examine our hearts, seek forgiveness, and extend grace to those who wrong us. Strengthen us to embody the love and compassion Jesus demonstrated in his betrayal. May our lives reflect your love and grace in all we do. Amen.

MAUNDY THURSDAY

Lectio Divina
John 13:1-17, 31b-35

Now before the festival of the Passover, Jesus knew that his hour had come to depart from this world and go to the Father. Having loved his own who were in the world, he loved them to the end. ² The devil had already put it into the heart of Judas son of Simon Iscariot to betray him. And during supper ³ Jesus, knowing that the Father had given all things into his hands, and that he had come from God and was going to God, ⁴ got up from the table, took off his outer robe, and tied a towel around himself. ⁵ Then he poured water into a basin and began to wash the disciples 'feet and to wipe them with the towel that was tied around him. ⁶ He came to Simon Peter, who said to him, "Lord, are you going to wash my feet?" ⁷ Jesus answered, "You do not know now what I am doing, but later you will understand." ⁸ Peter said to him, "You will never wash my feet." Jesus answered, "Unless I wash you, you have no share with me." ⁹ Simon Peter said to him, "Lord, not my feet only but also my hands and my head!" ¹⁰ Jesus said to him, "One who has bathed does not need to wash, except for the feet, but is entirely clean. And you are clean, though not all of you." ¹¹ For he knew who was to betray him; for this reason he said, "Not all of you are clean."

¹² After he had washed their feet, had put on his robe, and had returned to the table, he said to them, "Do you know what I have done to you? ¹³ You call me Teacher and Lord—and you are right, for that is what I am. ¹⁴ So if I, your Lord and Teacher, have washed your feet, you also ought to wash one another's feet. ¹⁵ For I have set you an example, that you also should do as I have done to you. ¹⁶ Very truly, I tell you, servants are not greater than their master, nor are messengers greater than the one who sent them. ¹⁷ If you know these things, you are blessed if you do them.

³¹ When he had gone out, Jesus said, "Now the Son of Man has been glorified, and God has been glorified in him. ³² If God has been glorified in him, God

will also glorify him in himself and will glorify him at once. [33] Little children, I am with you only a little longer. You will look for me; and as I said to the Jews so now I say to you, 'Where I am going, you cannot come. '[34] I give you a new commandment, that you love one another. Just as I have loved you, you also should love one another. [35] By this everyone will know that you are my disciples, if you have love for one another."

Visio Divina
"Jesus Washing the Feet of his Disciples" by Albert Edelfelt (1898)

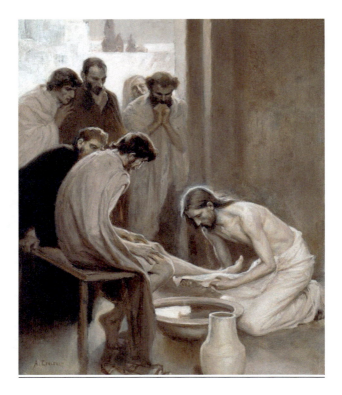

Poema Divina
"Service, Ritual, Redemption:Washing the Disciple s Feet" by Susan Noyes Anderson

To bathe soiled feet was but a servant's lot,
eschewed by men whose station lent them grace.
These did not stoop to take a lowly place,

nor pause to wonder if, one day, they ought.

Perhaps their privilege came to them unsought,

casting a veil of pride on every face,

miscasting tender service as disgrace

and glory as a prize that can be bought.

No matter. Man sees darkly, through a glass.

 Tis only One whose light our vision clears.

In Him, each blinding question that we ask

leads to a truth that vanquishes our fears.

Christ bathed His servants 'feet: a humble task,

then raised us all, washed clean in blood and tears.

Audio Divina
"Sacrifice of Song" by Mary Beth Philp

Daily Prayer
Father, Jesus amazes us! He set a true example by coming not to be served, but to serve. What an incredible display of humility and love! Help us understand the depth of his love and service in all we do. May we learn to set aside our pride and choose to love and serve others as he has loved and served us. Let our hearts reflect his compassion and grace in every interaction. Amen.

GOOD FRIDAY

Lectio Divina
John 18:1-19:37

18 After Jesus had spoken these words, he went out with his disciples across the Kidron valley to a place where there was a garden, which he and his disciples entered. ² Now Judas, who betrayed him, also knew the place, because Jesus often met there with his disciples. ³ So Judas brought a detachment of soldiers together with police from the chief priests and the Pharisees, and they came there with lanterns and torches and weapons. ⁴ Then Jesus, knowing all that was to happen to him, came forward and asked them, "Whom are you looking for?" ⁵ They answered, "Jesus of Nazareth." Jesus replied, "I am he." Judas, who betrayed him, was standing with them. ⁶ When Jesus said to them, "I am he," they stepped back and fell to the ground. ⁷ Again he asked them, "Whom are you looking for?" And they said, "Jesus of Nazareth." ⁸ Jesus answered, "I told you that I am he. So if you are looking for me, let these men go." ⁹ This was to fulfill the word that he had spoken, "I did not lose a single one of those whom you gave me." ¹⁰ Then Simon Peter, who had a sword, drew it, struck the high priest's slave, and cut off his right ear. The slave's name was Malchus. ¹¹ Jesus said to Peter, "Put your sword back into its sheath. Am I not to drink the cup that the Father has given me?"

¹² So the soldiers, their officer, and the Jewish police arrested Jesus and bound him. ¹³ First they took him to Annas, who was the father-in-law of Caiaphas, the high priest that year. ¹⁴ Caiaphas was the one who had advised the Jews that it was better to have one person die for the people.

¹⁵ Simon Peter and another disciple followed Jesus. Since that disciple was known to the high priest, he went with Jesus into the courtyard of the high priest, ¹⁶ but Peter was standing outside at the gate. So the other disciple, who was known to the high priest, went out, spoke to the woman who guarded the gate, and brought Peter in. ¹⁷ The woman said to Peter, "You are not also

one of this man's disciples, are you?" He said, "I am not." ¹⁸ Now the slaves and the police had made a charcoal fire because it was cold, and they were standing around it and warming themselves. Peter also was standing with them and warming himself.

¹⁹ Then the high priest questioned Jesus about his disciples and about his teaching. ²⁰ Jesus answered, "I have spoken openly to the world; I have always taught in synagogues and in the temple, where all the Jews come together. I have said nothing in secret. ²¹ Why do you ask me? Ask those who heard what I said to them; they know what I said." ²² When he had said this, one of the police standing nearby struck Jesus on the face, saying, "Is that how you answer the high priest?" ²³ Jesus answered, "If I have spoken wrongly, testify to the wrong. But if I have spoken rightly, why do you strike me?" ²⁴ Then Annas sent him bound to Caiaphas the high priest.

²⁵ Now Simon Peter was standing and warming himself. They asked him, "You are not also one of his disciples, are you?" He denied it and said, "I am not." ²⁶ One of the slaves of the high priest, a relative of the man whose ear Peter had cut off, asked, "Did I not see you in the garden with him?" ²⁷ Again Peter denied it, and at that moment the cock crowed.

²⁸ Then they took Jesus from Caiaphas to Pilate's headquarters. It was early in the morning. They themselves did not enter the headquarters, so as to avoid ritual defilement and to be able to eat the Passover. ²⁹ So Pilate went out to them and said, "What accusation do you bring against this man?" ³⁰ They answered, "If this man were not a criminal, we would not have handed him over to you." ³¹ Pilate said to them, "Take him yourselves and judge him according to your law." The Jews replied, "We are not permitted to put anyone to death." ³² (This was to fulfill what Jesus had said when he indicated the kind of death he was to die.)

³³ Then Pilate entered the headquarters again, summoned Jesus, and asked him, "Are you the King of the Jews?" ³⁴ Jesus answered, "Do you ask this on your own, or did others tell you about me?" ³⁵ Pilate replied, "I am not a Jew, am I? Your own nation and the chief priests have handed you over to me.

What have you done?" ³⁶ Jesus answered, "My kingdom is not from this world. If my kingdom were from this world, my followers would be fighting to keep me from being handed over to the Jews. But as it is, my kingdom is not from here." ³⁷ Pilate asked him, "So you are a king?" Jesus answered, "You say that I am a king. For this I was born, and for this I came into the world, to testify to the truth. Everyone who belongs to the truth listens to my voice." ³⁸ Pilate asked him, "What is truth?"

After he had said this, he went out to the Jews again and told them, "I find no case against him. ³⁹ But you have a custom that I release someone for you at the Passover. Do you want me to release for you the King of the Jews?" ⁴⁰ They shouted in reply, "Not this man, but Barabbas!" Now Barabbas was a bandit.

19 Then Pilate took Jesus and had him flogged. ² And the soldiers wove a crown of thorns and put it on his head, and they dressed him in a purple robe. ³ They kept coming up to him, saying, "Hail, King of the Jews!" and striking him on the face. ⁴ Pilate went out again and said to them, "Look, I am bringing him out to you to let you know that I find no case against him." ⁵ So Jesus came out, wearing the crown of thorns and the purple robe. Pilate said to them, "Here is the man!" ⁶ When the chief priests and the police saw him, they shouted, "Crucify him! Crucify him!" Pilate said to them, "Take him yourselves and crucify him; I find no case against him." ⁷ The Jews answered him, "We have a law, and according to that law he ought to die because he has claimed to be the Son of God."

⁸ Now when Pilate heard this, he was more afraid than ever. ⁹ He entered his headquarters again and asked Jesus, "Where are you from?" But Jesus gave him no answer. ¹⁰ Pilate therefore said to him, "Do you refuse to speak to me? Do you not know that I have power to release you, and power to crucify you?" ¹¹ Jesus answered him, "You would have no power over me unless it had been given you from above; therefore the one who handed me over to you is guilty of a greater sin." ¹² From then on Pilate tried to release him, but the Jews cried out, "If you release this man, you are no friend of the emperor. Everyone who claims to be a king sets himself against the emperor."

¹³ When Pilate heard these words, he brought Jesus outside and sat on the judge's bench at a place called The Stone Pavement, or in Hebrew Gabbatha. ¹⁴ Now it was the day of Preparation for the Passover; and it was about noon. He said to the Jews, "Here is your King!" ¹⁵ They cried out, "Away with him! Away with him! Crucify him!" Pilate asked them, "Shall I crucify your King?" The chief priests answered, "We have no king but the emperor." ¹⁶ Then he handed him over to them to be crucified.

So they took Jesus; ¹⁷ and carrying the cross by himself, he went out to what is called The Place of the Skull, which in Hebrew is called Golgotha. ¹⁸ There they crucified him, and with him two others, one on either side, with Jesus between them. ¹⁹ Pilate also had an inscription written and put on the cross. It read, "Jesus of Nazareth, the King of the Jews." ²⁰ Many of the Jews read this inscription, because the place where Jesus was crucified was near the city; and it was written in Hebrew, in Latin, and in Greek. ²¹ Then the chief priests of the Jews said to Pilate, "Do not write, 'The King of the Jews, 'but, 'This man said, I am King of the Jews. " '²² Pilate answered, "What I have written I have written." ²³ When the soldiers had crucified Jesus, they took his clothes and divided them into four parts, one for each soldier. They also took his tunic; now the tunic was seamless, woven in one piece from the top. ²⁴ So they said to one another, "Let us not tear it, but cast lots for it to see who will get it." This was to fulfill what the scripture says,

"They divided my clothes among themselves,
    and for my clothing they cast lots."

²⁵ And that is what the soldiers did. Meanwhile, standing near the cross of Jesus were his mother, and his mother's sister, Mary the wife of Clopas, and Mary Magdalene. ²⁶ When Jesus saw his mother and the disciple whom he loved standing beside her, he said to his mother, "Woman, here is your son." ²⁷ Then he said to the disciple, "Here is your mother." And from that hour the disciple took her into his own home.

28 After this, when Jesus knew that all was now finished, he said (in order to fulfill the scripture), "I am thirsty." 29 A jar full of sour wine was standing there. So they put a sponge full of the wine on a branch of hyssop and held it to his mouth. 30 When Jesus had received the wine, he said, "It is finished." Then he bowed his head and gave up his spirit.

31 Since it was the day of Preparation, the Jews did not want the bodies left on the cross during the sabbath, especially because that sabbath was a day of great solemnity. So they asked Pilate to have the legs of the crucified men broken and the bodies removed. 32 Then the soldiers came and broke the legs of the first and of the other who had been crucified with him. 33 But when they came to Jesus and saw that he was already dead, they did not break his legs. 34 Instead, one of the soldiers pierced his side with a spear, and at once blood and water came out. 35 (He who saw this has testified so that you also may believe. His testimony is true, and he knows that he tells the truth.) 36 These things occurred so that the scripture might be fulfilled, "None of his bones shall be broken." 37 And again another passage of scripture says, "They will look on the one whom they have pierced."

Visio Divina
"The Crucifixion" by Bartolomé Estebán Murillo (1675)

Poema Divina
"Alas! and Did My Savior Bleed " by Isaac Watts

Alas! and did my Saviour bleed,
  And did my sov'reign die?
Would he devote that sacred Head
  For such a Worm as I?

Thy Body slain, sweet Jesus, thine,

And bath'd in its own Blood,
While all expos'd to Wrath divine
  The glorious Sufferer stood?

Was it for Crimes that I had done
  He groan'd upon the Tree?
Amazing Pity! Grace unknown!
  And Love beyond Degree?

Well might the Sun in Darkness hide,
  And shut his Glories in,
When God the mighty Maker died
  For Man the Creatures Sin.

Thus might I hide my blushing Face
  While his dear Cross appears,
Dissolve my Heart in Thankfulness,
  And melt mine Eyes to Tears.

But Drops of Grief can ne'er repay
  The Debt of Love I owe;
Here, Lord, I give my self away,
  'Tis all that I can do.

Audio Divina
"For The Cross" by Brian & Jenn Johnson

Daily Prayer
Behold the Lamb of God, who takes away the sin of the world. Father, You allowed
Jesus to endure betrayal, injustice, and unimaginable suffering to bring forgiveness
and redemption to us all. Through his sacrifice, we are invited into a life of grace and
reconciliation. May we live in gratitude, reflecting his love to others. It is finished!
Hallelujah, what a Savior! Amen.

HOLY SATURDAY

__Lectio Divina__
John 19:38-42

³⁸ After these things, Joseph of Arimathea, who was a disciple of Jesus, though a secret one because of his fear of the Jews, asked Pilate to let him take away the body of Jesus. Pilate gave him permission; so he came and removed his body. ³⁹ Nicodemus, who had at first come to Jesus by night, also came, bringing a mixture of myrrh and aloes, weighing about a hundred pounds. ⁴⁰ They took the body of Jesus and wrapped it with the spices in linen cloths, according to the burial custom of the Jews. ⁴¹ Now there was a garden in the place where he was crucified, and in the garden there was a new tomb in which no one had ever been laid. ⁴² And so, because it was the Jewish day of Preparation, and the tomb was nearby, they laid Jesus there.

__Visio Divina__
"Mosaic of the Burial of Jesus Christ Showing Jesus Taken down from the Cross" by Godong (2018)

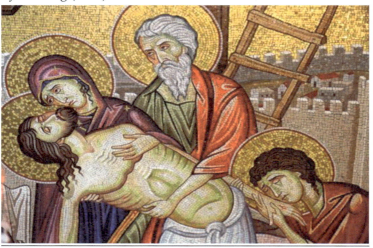

"Up from the Grave He Arose" verses 1 & 2 by Daniel Thornton

Low in the grave He lay
Jesus my Savior!
Waiting the coming day
Jesus my Lord!

Vainly they watch His bed
Jesus, my Savior!
Vainly they seal the dead
Jesus my Lord!

Audio Divina
"Grave" by Cochren & Co.

Daily Prayer
Father, our hearts are burdened today by the saddening reality of Jesus '
burial. If it all ends here, we are lost and without hope. How could we have
ever imagined our Savior laid in a tomb? We bring our brokenness and
sorrow to you, crying out for you to come near to us in our grief. Thank you
for the assurance that even in this place, you come near. Amen.

The Examen
1. What part of this week's devotional stood out to you? How did it
    impact your prayers and spiritual growth?
2. How did you handle challenges or moments of inspiration this week?
    Did they encourage you to take a new step in your faith?
3. How has this week's practice helped you understand Lent and prepare
    for Easter? Has your view of sacrifice, repentance, or forgiveness
    changed?
4. Are there any distractions or habits you'd like to let go of to make Lent
    more meaningful? How will you plan to create a peaceful, reflective
    space for yourself each day?

Lectio Divina
John 20:1-18

Early on the first day of the week, while it was still dark, Mary Magdalene came to the tomb and saw that the stone had been removed from the tomb. [2] So she ran and went to Simon Peter and the other disciple, the one whom Jesus loved, and said to them, "They have taken the Lord out of the tomb, and we do not know where they have laid him." [3] Then Peter and the other disciple set out and went toward the tomb. [4] The two were running together, but the other disciple outran Peter and reached the tomb first. [5] He bent down to look in and saw the linen wrappings lying there, but he did not go in. [6] Then Simon Peter came, following him, and went into the tomb. He saw the linen wrappings lying there, [7] and the cloth that had been on Jesus 'head, not lying with the linen wrappings but rolled up in a place by itself. [8] Then the other disciple, who reached the tomb first, also went in, and he saw and believed; [9] for as yet they did not understand the scripture, that he must rise from the dead. [10] Then the disciples returned to their homes.

[11] But Mary stood weeping outside the tomb. As she wept, she bent over to look into the tomb; [12] and she saw two angels in white, sitting where the body of Jesus had been lying, one at the head and the other at the feet. [13] They said to her, "Woman, why are you weeping?" She said to them, "They have taken away my Lord, and I do not know where they have laid him." [14] When she had said this, she turned around and saw Jesus standing there, but she did not know that it was Jesus. [15] Jesus said to her, "Woman, why are you weeping? Whom are you looking for?" Supposing him to be the gardener, she said to him, "Sir, if you have carried him away, tell me where you have laid him, and I will take him away." [16] Jesus said to her, "Mary!" She turned and said to him in Hebrew, "Rabbouni!" (which means Teacher). [17] Jesus said to her, "Do not hold on to me, because I have not yet ascended to the Father. But go to my brothers and say to them, 'I am ascending to my Father and your Father, to my God and your God. " '[18] Mary Magdalene went and

announced to the disciples, "I have seen the Lord"; and she told them that he had said these things to her.

Visio Divina
"Resurrection Painting" by Bill Bell (2000)

Poema Divina
"Christ the Lord Is Risen Today" by Charles Wesley

Christ the Lord is ris n today, Alleluia!

Sons of men and angels say, Alleluia!

Raise your joys and triumphs high, Alleluia!

Sing, ye heav ns, and earth, reply, Alleluia!

Lives again our glorious King, Alleluia!

Where, O death, is now thy sting? Alleluia!

Once He died our souls to save, Alleluia!

Where thy victory, O grave? Alleluia

Love s redeeming work is done, Alleluia!

Fought the fight, the battle won, Alleluia!

Death in vain forbids His rise, Alleluia!

Christ hath opened paradise, Alleluia

Soar we now where Christ hath led, Alleluia!

Foll wing our exalted Head, Alleluia!

Made like Him, like Him we rise, Alleluia!

Ours the cross, the grave, the skies, Alleluia

Hail the Lord of earth and heaven, Alleluia!

Praise to Thee by both be given, Alleluia!

Thee we greet triumphant now, Alleluia!

Hail the Resurrection, thou, Alleluia

King of glory, Soul of bliss, Alleluia!

Everlasting life is this, Alleluia!

Thee to know, Thy pow r to prove, Alleluia!

Thus to sing, and thus to love, Alleluia!

Audio Divina
"Forever" by Kari Jobe

Daily Prayer
Christ is risen!

Your rising from the grave seals the final victory over sin and death. You have broken every chain and offer new, abundant, and eternal life to all who believe. Let our lives each day bear witness to the power of your resurrection and the hope you offer to the world you created.

Christ is risen indeed!
Hallelujah!
Amen.

Made in the USA
Columbia, SC
21 March 2025

55476303R00100